MW00738032

THIS BOOK WILL TEACH YOU TO

OWN YOUR TIME

THE INSIDER'S GUIDE TO MASTERING TIME MANAGEMENT

WHALEN
BOOK · WORKS

"THE BAD NEWS
IS TIME FLIES. THE
GOOD NEWS IS
YOU'RE THE PILOT."

—MICHAEL ALTSHULER

CONTENTS

INTRODUCTION. 6

**CHAPTER 1: WE ALL
NEED MORE TIME 8**

What Is Time? 10

Time Flies! Why Time Seems
to Speed Up. 12

Why Multitasking Isn't All It's
Cracked Up to Be 14

The Importance of Planning
Your Day: Six Reasons 17

Six Ways to Establish
Routines 19

To Do Lists: Yes or No? 21

"Chunking" Time. 23

How to Use Technology to
Help You Manage Your Time . . . 26

**CHAPTER 2: TIME
MANAGEMENT AT
WORK 29**

Eight Tips for Getting Ready
for Work in the Morning 30

Seven Suggestions for
Planning Your Commute. 34

Six Tips When Making a
Daily Schedule 37

Five Ideas to Prioritize
Your Work Tasks. 40

Eight Actions for
Prioritizing Emails 43

Seven Tips for Efficient
Work Organization 46

Seven Ways to Set Realistic
Goals That You Can
Actually Meet. 49

Breaking Down Big
Jobs to Smaller,
Manageable Ones. 52

Delegating and Sharing
Work Tasks 55

Six Ways of Adding Variety
to Your Work 58

Seven Ways to Make
Meetings More Efficient 60

Is Working from Home
for You?. 63

Don't Overextend
Yourself! 66

**CHAPTER 3: TIME
MANAGEMENT IN
YOUR PERSONAL
LIFE. 69**

Nine Ways to Make
Time for Yourself 70

Making Time for Friends
and Family: Seven Ways 74

Seven Time Management
Tips for Everyday Chores
and Errands 78

How to Make the Most
of Your Nights 81

How to Make the Most
of Your Weekends 85

Knowing When to
Take a Vacation 89

Watching for Signs of
Stress in the Body 92

Keeping an Eye on
Your Sleep Patterns
and Mental State 95

CHAPTER 4:
PROCRASTINATION:
THE GREAT ENEMY . . . 102

Why We Procrastinate;
It May Not Be Why
You Think 104

The Effects of Ongoing
Procrastination 107

Ten Ways to Watch Out
for Boredom! 110

How to Beat the
Procrastination Problem:
Ten Strategies 114

Five Ways to Meet
Deadlines without
the Stress 118

The Online Time-Wasting
Scourge and How to
Recognize It 120

Learning to Disconnect
from the Online World 124

RESOURCES. 132

Further Reading. 133

Online Resources
for Mental Health Issues 135

About the Author. 137

INDEX 138

ABOUT THE
PUBLISHER 144

INTRODUCTION

This Book Will Teach You to Own Your Time tackles one of the key things we never seem to have enough of: time. Increasingly, our days seem jam-packed with one task after another, and not just at work; our personal lives don't seem to be our own, and the time away from work is all too often spent doing things we need to do rather than what we want to do. We find ourselves wondering, "Where did the day (or the weekend, or the week, or the month, or the year!) go?" Surprisingly, a good amount of our time gets wasted in ways we may not even be aware of. Learning to spot those distractions and minimize them can go a long way toward helping you reclaim your time for you!

Whether you are a student, an employee at a company, or just someone who needs to get back on top of time, this brief book will offer you tools, tips, and techniques to make the most of your days and nights. You'll learn to make and keep schedules, use technology to your advantage instead of letting it rule you (cough! Social media, cough!), and understand why we procrastinate and fritter away so many precious hours. Understanding the why of time wasting goes a long way to putting a stop to it. If you're feeling overworked at your job, you'll learn ways to cope and prioritize, and if your personal life is a temporal shambles, this book will help you pull it back in and make you a master of time!

The book is divided into four chapters grouped by subject. Each chapter gives you basic information and steps to get started.

Use each chapter as a reference and guide when you want to look up a specific topic. Feel free to dip into the book wherever you like, and read chapters in any order that works for you. Some portions of the book may be more relevant to you than others, but there is something here for everyone who wants to learn how to better manage their time. A book this size gives you a summary, and you can use it as a starting point for further learning and background research. This book is not a substitute for legal or medical advice, and if you need further help on any of the topics here, there are tips so you can seek it out on your own. The Resources section at the end of the book offers helpful further reading, and a list of websites will give you links for help regarding mental health issues. This book is your introduction to how to take back control of your life and own your time!

CHAPTER 1

WE ALL NEED MORE TIME

These days, everyone seems to worry about not having enough time. We're always too busy to do many of the things we'd like to do. In fact, we've made "busy" a kind of go-to word for describing our lives: "How are you? Oh, good; busy, but good." The cult of busyness seems to be something on which everyone thrives, or tries to; we use it as an excuse all the time: "Sorry I couldn't make it last night; I was too busy."

If we don't have enough to do, we start to feel inadequate or unproductive. If others see us as not having enough to do, we may feel guilty for not being busy enough or worry that we'll be judged. The problem with all this busyness is that there simply aren't enough hours in the day to be as busy as we think we're supposed to be and still have enough time to do everything. This devotion to doing things nonstop can lead us to neglect ourselves. We start losing sleep, we skip lunch, we work late—and this behavior is a long-term recipe for disaster.

This chapter looks at time: what it is and how we can start rethinking how we approach it. If you're feeling overtaxed and time-short, here is some advice to start getting your time back under your control, where it belongs.

> **"Short as life is, we make it still shorter by the careless waste of time."**
>
> **—VICTOR HUGO**

WHAT IS TIME?

This is deep question, but don't worry, we're not going to delve into a philosophy discussion or an astrophysics lesson! Time is something of an inscrutable mystery, anyway. There are mathematical arguments that it can run both forward and backward, that it's related to space and gravity ("space-time" was long ago theorized by people far smarter than average!), and several other fascinating if mind-boggling theories. Time can even be experienced differently depending on the speed one is traveling and one's location!

For us in our everyday lives, it's enough to know that it marches forever forward and there's nothing we can do about that. Obviously, we all know what time is, since we experience it constantly, but how can we start to think about it in ways that can be more useful to us? Here are some important points to remember about your own time.

- **Time exists right now.** The past has already happened, and the future is still to be determined. It may seem to be a very Zen philosophy, but the only time that truly exists is now. Dwelling on past mistakes and regrets or fretting too much about the future will not get you anywhere. Work to correct the mistakes of the past, while planning for the future, but always remember that the only time you can do either of those things is now.

- **Time cannot be controlled.** Time progresses at the same pace, no matter how much we don't want it to. The pace can seem relentless, as we ask ourselves how something happened a year, five years, or ten years ago. We age, our friends and family age, things change, and while we'd all love to slow things down a bit, it doesn't happen. The seconds tick away.

- **Time vanishes.** Time is very much ephemeral, while paradoxically it's always with us. The moment is here and then gone, vanished into history and memory, always to be replaced by a new moment. When we're on a great vacation, on the perfect date, or doing something else we love, we want it to last forever, but of course, it never does. We must remember to savor each moment and event—and experience them fully.

- **Time has value, even if we don't see it.** How often do we look back on things and wish we'd spent more time doing something, or not wasted time on doing something else? Let's be honest, we do it very often. We don't seem to appreciate the value of the moment in the moment itself, and then we reminisce about it, wishing we'd done things differently. If only we could focus more on those moments in the now, and less after they're gone!

> **"Time is a created thing. To say 'I don't have time,' is like saying, 'I don't want to.'"**
>
> **—LAO TZU**

TIME FLIES! WHY TIME SEEMS TO SPEED UP

For many, time to seems to speed up as we get older. The reality is that we still have the same twenty-four hours a day that we always did, but it's how we approach them that's different. Why does it seem like time goes by so fast? There are a number of theories.

Time may always progress at the same pace (on Earth, anyway), but our sense of it can definitely change according to our circumstances. How often has a dreary day at work seemed never to end, while a fantastic day out is over all too soon? Our subjective experience of time plays into this. We don't have an internal clock ticking off the seconds, so the passage of time can feel more fluid than clocklike.

One conversation many people have is how time does appear to speed up as we age. Part of this has to do with how we perceive time in relation to our own lives. For a child of seven, a year of their life is a significant portion, whereas for someone who is seventy, a year is not even 2 percent of their life. Those early years of living are also spent processing so many new things that impress on the brain and the memory, while in later years we will probably have fewer novel experiences. As neurologist Santosh Kesari notes: "We gauge time by memorable events and fewer new things occur as we age to remember, making it seem like childhood lasted longer."

Another theory suggests that time seems to progress so swiftly because our heads are always stuck in the future. As a society, we've collectively convinced ourselves that tomorrow is better than today, next month is better than this month, and that by next year, we'll really be in the place we want to be. We have a vacation coming up in June, two weeks off at the holidays, a great party to go to on Saturday night. When all of these things arrive, then our lives will be better! But these events come and go, and we're forced to look forward to the next big thing, all the while forgetting that we live in the now and are ignoring it because the "then" is obviously so much better. Can you see how this starts to make us ignore the present and wish it would go away?

Our working lives are very much affected by this. The workday is usually structured around the 9-to-5 model. We dread Mondays and maybe joke about them on social media, feel optimistic when we've gotten to Wednesday (the "hump day" of the week), and then cheer when Friday finally arrives. Unfortunately, that leaves us just two days to get everything else done that we wanted or needed to do, only to then start the whole cycle over again next Monday. Is this the best model? Is this the best use of our time?

We may be resigned to this being just the way things are. The idea of just "getting through the day" is something that we all subscribe to in one way or another. But as Seth Godin writes: "Is tomorrow another day to get through? After you get through all the days, then what happens?"

What happens, indeed? How can we make better use of time, so that it doesn't seem to sail by or be wasted? We'll discuss this more later in the book.

[

"Time is what we want most, but what we use worst."

—WILLIAM PENN

]

It used to be believed that multitasking, the idea of juggling two or more tasks at once, could be an effective way to be more productive and save time. In fact, research shows that nothing could be further from the truth. Trying to work on things simultaneously or in rapid succession back and forth pretty much guarantees that you'll do nothing right, and may even harm you in the long run. And you certainly won't save much, if any, time. Let's look at some of the facts, so that you can confidently say no to this unwise practice.

- **Very few people can do it.** One study of a driving simulation that also required other auditory attention found that "2.5 percent of the sample showed absolutely no performance decrements with respect to performing single and dual tasks." That's a very small number. Now, you may be thinking this was for driving, and your work isn't so demanding or dangerous, but the point was to look at how the brain is able to divide up simultaneous tasks, and except for those few superheroes, not many people were good at it. You might be a part of that 2.5 percent, but you have to admit there's a good chance that you're not.

- **Switching between projects is no better.** Other studies have shown that focusing on one task for a bit and then flipping over to another task didn't work very well either. So, even if you take a little time to do one thing and then try working on another, you may be disappointed with the results.

- **Technology is making things worse.** Smart phones, tablets, earbuds, "busy" websites . . . so many electronic things are vying for our attention that we often feel compelled to plug into several at once, and our focus gets shot all over the place. This scatterbrain approach, where everything is screeching to be noticed, is not doing our head or our health any good. Trying to talk on a headset with a client while also typing up an unrelated report just means you're going to do both jobs poorly, which may have a bad outcome for your work.

- **Multitasking affects brain activity negatively.** Trying to focus on more than one thing at once actually leads to reduced activity in the brain areas devoted to paying attention. In short, the more you try to take in, the less you will comprehend and remember. We're just not wired that way. And the more you try to do it, the worse you get; it's not something you can practice and improve. A study at Stanford University found that those who thought they were doing well and that multitasking was making them more efficient actually did worse.

- **Multitasking lowers IQ.** Whatever the merits of the IQ score, a University of London study discovered that trying to juggle two or more mental tasks at once over a period of time had the same effect on IQ as substantial sleep loss. In other words, it's not good!

- **The consequences can linger after the event.** The problem with regular multitasking, as the Stanford study showed, is not just that it lowers your productivity while doing multiple tasks; it can affect how you work even when not juggling two or more items at once. Researcher

Clifford Nass noted: "We studied people who were chronic multitaskers, and even when we did not ask them to do anything close to the level of multitasking they were doing, their cognitive processes were impaired. So basically, they are worse at most of the kinds of thinking not only required for multitasking but what we generally think of as involving deep thought." The solution to this is to stop multitasking.

- **What about music?** Can you listen to music while working? Everyone does it. The answer is probably yes, with some qualifications. If you're listening to something that's fairly mellow and nonintrusive, you might find that it helps you relax and puts you in a better state. But energetic music, especially with vocals, will probably at least distract you, if not impair whatever it is you're trying to concentrate on. If you're trying to write a report and pop lyrics keep ringing in your ears, it'll be like having someone talking at you. Mellow instrumental jazz, ambient sounds, and Chopin? Probably fine. Techno, hip-hop, or death metal? Wait until you get home!

- **Limit what you do.** The research seems to indicate that you should never work on more than two things at once, if at all possible, and that if you can, try to devote at least twenty minutes at a time to one project before moving on to the next. By choosing to mono-task and devote your attention to one project only, you'll make better use of your time and likely feel less tired at the end of the day!

THE IMPORTANCE OF PLANNING YOUR DAY: SIX REASONS

If you just go through the day or the week (or life) flailing around with no plan, you'll get frustrated and worn out pretty quickly. One of the key ways to manage your time comes from starting each day with a plan, for both work and your personal life. This doesn't mean that you need to have everything spelled out in agonizing detail, but having a good overall structure will make you happier and better prepared. There will always be unexpected happenings, but you can be as ready as possible. Here are some of the benefits of planning.

1. **You'll reduce your stress.** This is probably the most important reason. Worrying about what might come up with no plan in place to face it will give you sleepless nights, indigestion, and potentially other health complaints.

2. **You'll be prepared.** Knowing what's ahead in the office or whatever your job might be will give you a better chance to be ready for it. You'll never be able to anticipate everything, of course, but at least you have a plan in place.

3. **You'll be able to track your progress.** With a good plan in place, you'll be able to see how well you did at the end of the day, and if you're keeping to your schedule or getting off somehow.

4. You'll understand yourself better. Having a plan is a great way to see how you'll act on it, and if you can follow your own orders. If you have a tendency to get off track, ignore your own recommendations, or otherwise fail to live up to your plan, you'll be able to identify some areas that you should work on.

5. You'll feel more motivated. Having a plan can give you the motivation you need, whereas just sliding through the day might not be very inspiring.

6. You'll be able to prioritize. By having a solid plan, you'll see what's wasting your time and what you should be focusing on instead. But beware: if you take a good look at it, checking social media constantly might suddenly look like the waste of time it actually is! You might just end up making some really useful and long-lasting changes.

> **"The man who is prepared has his battle half fought."**
>
> **—MIGUEL DE CERVANTES**

SIX WAYS TO ESTABLISH ROUTINES

A routine is a kind of habit; in this case, it's a good one that you want to follow. Establishing good habits about your time can take some work, but it's worth making the effort. You'll gain a greater sense of control over your schedule and be more prepared for whatever happens. Here are some tips for making good changes and choices.

1. **List your daily to-dos.** Every day you'll have some things that need to be taken care of, no matter what else comes up. Write these down in any order, as they come to you. Even simply things like eating breakfast and brushing your teeth. The point is to get everything down. It can be helpful to handwrite this information down in a small notebook, instead of typing it up on your laptop or phone. The sensation of writing by hand is more visceral and feels more real. You can also keep your notepad with you and add things to it as you think of them.

2. **Think about when you are at your best.**
   Some people are natural early risers and rush out to meet the day before sunrise. Others like to stay awake into the night, when they really come alive. You'll already know where you fit on this sliding scale. If you have a 9-to-5 job, your rising and sleeping times will already be chosen for you, regardless of what hours you prefer. But even within that framework, you'll know if you do some things better in the morning or the afternoon. If possible, be thinking about how you can shuffle around some of your work tasks to the time when you are in the best state of mind to address them.

3. **Specify times.** Try to create a schedule that gets into detail, now that you have a list of your daily to-dos. This is especially helpful in the morning when you are preparing to go to work or to do whatever tasks you have to do. Set a time for waking up and stick to it. Eat breakfast at the same time, shower (unless you prefer to do that the night before), prepare to leave your home. Stick to the same times for these every morning. If you have some flexibility at work, try to work on the same things at the same time each day. All of this may seem a bit monotonous, but it will help you establish ideal times.

4. **Maintain some flexibility.** Your evenings might be a bit more flexible. You may not always eat at the same time or do the same things each night, and this is as it should be. It's fine to build in some flexible scheduling to your personal time. But the unexpected may also happen at work. You may prefer to work on a specific task at 11:00 a.m. every morning, but something else comes up, so you have to set it aside. You're never going to have the exact same schedule every day, so be prepared for changes here and there.

5. **Use evenings to prepare for the next day.** Use your evening time for yourself and/or your family, but also set aside some time to make sure that everything is in order for tomorrow. This might include making lunch, laying out your clothes, reviewing anything important for the morning's work, and so on.

6. **Practice your routine.** Now that you have a plan, put it into action! Try out your new routine for several days and see what works and what doesn't. You may need to tweak some things here and there, but it's all about finding out what works best for you. Once you have it to your liking, commit to your routine for at least thirty days. The point here is to get you in the habit of following the same routine so that it feels natural.

TO-DO LISTS: YES OR NO?

The answer to this question is a definite yes! If you're establishing a routine, you've already read about making a to-do list. In fact, it's good to have more than one. Create a daily to-do list for all of these things that you'll be repeating each day, and individual lists tailored to each day or week that focus on specific tasks and projects that need to be completed by a certain time. Don't just make it a one-line reminder; get detailed so that you won't forget anything important. Making these kinds of lists is a good plan for both your professional and personal lives; knowing what you need to do over the weekend can be just as important as your tasks at work. Here are some of the benefits of a good to-do list.

- **It brings a sense of structure and order.** Seeing everything that you need to do all laid out gives you an overview that can make everything seem less daunting.

- **You can prioritize.** Not everything needs your attention right away or all at once. With a good list, you can prioritize those tasks that are most urgent or have looming deadlines, and manage them with more confidence.

- **It gets it all out of your head.** Trying to remember everything you have to do can be a confusing pain. A good, detailed list helps you keep track of all your responsibilities and ensures you won't forget them . . . unless you forgot to add something to begin with, of course!

- **It makes you accountable.** Once a task is written down and you have a reminder of it, you have to attend to it, no excuses! You can't tell yourself you forgot or conveniently put it aside until later. Making a list and forcing yourself to commit to it will ensure everything gets done.

- **It gives you a sense of accomplishment.** As you check off items on your list, it will feel great! In fact, it might spur you to get things done sooner, if you can see the progress you're making. There's a definite psychological boost to seeing yourself work through a list of tasks and actually doing them. You'll feel more productive.

- **It can give you more control over your time.** As you work through a daily list, it might be that some tasks will be finished sooner than you expected. This frees up your time for other things, or maybe even taking a short break early. Hooray!

- **It will help you feel more in control.** An itemized list breaks things down into bite-size chunks and can give you a sense of being on top of it all, rather than being swamped. Always look to break tasks down to smaller sizes and components. That way, you'll never have to worry about forgetting something important. Studies have shown that unfinished tasks tend to nag at us, and can make us anxious and stressed.

- **It can motivate you.** Seeing things set down and divided up can reduce the feeling of some task or project being overwhelming and instead show that it's possible to make a start and really finish it. As with the sense of accomplishment when you check things off, a list can get you in the right frame of mind to continue on with the next task.

"CHUNKING" TIME

Chunking can be seen as an alternative, if not the direct opposite, of multitasking. Instead of trying to do multiple tasks at once and doing them all poorly, you can instead set out "chunks" of time to do similar tasks and focus only on those. This works for both your personal and professional needs. Here is how to go about it.

For time chunking (such as at work):

1. **Write down all your tasks.** This is like the to-do list, but you'll see the difference in moment. In this case, don't just do a brain dump of everything onto the page; put the most important items first and work down to the ones that can wait until later.

2. **Block out your time in sections.** Estimate how long each task will take to complete, or at least how long you can concentrate on it at any one time. Set aside chunks of time to work on those tasks, and only those tasks. Some studies suggest being aware of what times of day you feel most productive, and scheduling the biggest and most complex tasks for then. If there are deadlines proscribed by your workplace as to when things need to be done, your mood may not matter. Whatever needs to be done first, needs to be done first.

3. **Work only on that task at the allotted time.** If at all possible, give your attention only to that task or project at that time. Obviously, sometimes you'll have interruptions— an important phone call or an urgent email—but as much as possible, try to block outside distractions and devote your time

to the task at hand. If you need to, let your coworkers know that you need some uninterrupted time. The goal is to be focused on it and get as much done and done well in the time you've set aside for it.

4. **Commit to your plan as much as possible.** The point is not to deviate from the plan if you can help it. When you have your time set aside, work on that project. When the time is up, try to switch to your next task, unless there is an important reason to keep going, such as a deadline by the end of the day, a problem you're on the verge of solving, or something similar. This is especially good for multiday bigger tasks, where it's OK to set it aside and move on.

5. **Consider starting small.** The idea of chunking all of your time may be intimidating at first, especially if you don't have a good sense of how long each task will take. A good way to incorporate this method into your daily work practice is to start smaller. Set aside a time chunk for one task and see how it goes. Can you get it done (or what you need to at the moment) in the time you gave yourself? With a bit of practice, you'll be able to judge how long different tasks will take and can adjust your schedule accordingly, and add in more time chunks.

For errand chunking (such as in your personal life):

Time chunking can be valuable in your home life as well, especially if you find yourself being very busy and needing to get a lot done on, say, a Saturday, because the rest of the workweek is filled up. But another kind of chunking revolves around grouping together tasks based on similarities. Here is how to go about it.

1. **Write down all your tasks and errands.** This time, you can ignore the order of importance. A lot of that is subjective anyway: Which is more important, getting coffee or doing laundry? All right, that was a bad example; coffee always comes first!

2. **Look for commonalities.** Which tasks are related geographically? Which are related by subject? Try to find ways to separate them out.

3. **Group together all common tasks.** Getting your coffee from the local shop may coincide with needing to drop off an important letter at the post office. The place where you buy cat food might be two blocks away from your dentist's office. All of this might seem obvious in your head, but it makes more sense when you see it written down. Now, instead of ten small tasks, you may have three groups or sets of tasks that are all related. That's a lot easier to envision!

4. **Commit to doing related tasks in the same chunk of time.** Do everything you can in that group in the same portion of time, if at all possible. You'll probably be surprised at how much time it can save.

All of this advice may seem completely obvious, but it's remarkable how many people don't take these steps and find themselves being run ragged. Chunking tasks and errands this way will be the most efficient use of your time, and may even give you a few extra hours when everything is done.

HOW TO USE TECHNOLOGY TO HELP YOU MANAGE YOUR TIME

Despite a commitment to improving time use, it's fair to say that we could all use a little help! Thankfully, there are any number of good technological items and gadgets that can assist you in owning your time and getting on top of everything you do. Specific programs and apps come and go, and there is always some new craze, but here are some general suggestions that can give you a helping hand.

- **Use a calendar.** Pretty much every email program has some kind of calendar built into it. These are invaluable for keeping track of your tasks, necessary meetings, and so on. Most often, they can be synced up with your mobile device, so you'll have access to them whenever you need to. Your team may have a group calendar that keeps bigger project tasks and milestones carefully recorded.

- **Use a file-sharing program.** There are many good ones out there, and chances are your company already has a program they prefer. The advantages of these, of course, is to ensure that everyone has access to group files and can review or make changes as needed, without everything having to be emailed or sent around for review.

- **Find the apps that suit you.** A simple internet search reveals a bewildering number of apps devoted to efficiency and time management. It's not this book's purpose to recommend specific apps, since these are constantly changing and being updated. Some are better, some will stand the test of time (slight pun intended!), while others won't. You'll need to go through lists of these and find the ones that best suit you and your needs. But you can find apps for just about everything: task lists and reminders; personal calendars; apps for making notes, syncing your files, and creating to-do lists; meditation and concentration-boosting apps; and more!

- **Use a password encryption program.** How often have you gone back to something you haven't used in a while, found that the password is not saved, and you have no idea what it is? But you *really* need to get in? The solution to this is not to use the same password for every site (a **very** bad idea), but to make use of a password manager. Your passwords will be stored in an encrypted database, much safer than you writing everything down on a card or some similar method. Using this kind of service will save you time and worry.

- **Don't be overcommitted to tech.** Your company may use Slack or a similar program so that everyone can interact and get feedback quickly, but be careful about the amount of time you put into it. At the end of the day, when you log off, is it *really* the end of the day? Are you expected to keep reading and replying to messages on your own time? Find out what company and departmental policies about this are. Taking work home with you may be necessary in some cases, but if you're constantly being expected to check in and review things in the evening before the next day, ask yourself if you're being paid enough and if they're respecting your time. Just because others want to be workaholics doesn't mean that you should follow along. Getting addicted to the job is a great way to burn out fast, and technology can be an easy way to let this happen.

- **Limit social media.** This is one technology that won't do you any good. Unless your job is specifically using social media for marketing, advertising and other jobs, keeping your eyes off it will serve you better in the long run. Some estimates now say that the average person will spend five years of their life on various social media sites. Five years! Ask yourself if that time couldn't be better spent somewhere else: with friends and family, working on your own career goals, getting extra work done to save time and stress later, even developing yourself in other ways (fitness, meditation, cooking, whatever you're into). Social media can be fun in small amounts, but various studies now point to its many negative effects, too. See "The Online Time-Wasting Scourge and How to Recognize It" on page 120 for more tips on limiting your exposure. Social media is one technology that will **not** help you use your time better!

> "It's not enough to be busy, so are the ants. The question is, what are we busy about?"
>
> **—HENRY DAVID THOREAU**

CHAPTER 2

TIME MANAGEMENT AT WORK

It pretty much goes without saying that you need to be on top of your time at work. With expectations, deadlines, team projects, meetings, and so much more, it can seem like your entire day is based around moving from one time slot to another. Just getting into work on time in the morning can seem like a slog some days. Taking control of your time at work (at least as much as possible) is a big deal, and will let you feel less stressed, more productive, and more in control. It will also show you off in a good light to your boss and superiors; successful time management is a key to career advancement. This chapter goes into detail about ways you can make your work time work better for you.

EIGHT TIPS FOR GETTING READY FOR WORK IN THE MORNING

Getting up at the crack of the alarm, dashing about, showering, eating breakfast, and getting yourself out the door can be highly stressful and unpleasant, and not just on Mondays! Starting the day off wrong can mess up the whole day, so you want to be sure that you get things done right. If you're struggling to get up and go, if you're always worrying about being late, if everything is chaotic and unready, here are some useful tips to get back in control of your work mornings (or any mornings) and make the most of the time you have. Mornings don't need to be the stressful events that most fear, and with a bit of practice, you'll feel much better about when the sun comes up.

1. **Get ready the night before.** Have the clothes you want to wear all ready (at least hanging in the front of your closet or wardrobe), have any materials you need to take with you prepared and placed by the door, have your lunch made (if you're taking it), have the shoes you're going to wear set out. Make sure you have your bus or train pass if you're using one, or make sure your car has enough gasoline. Check the weather the night before, and have any rain or snow gear ready. Basically, just be prepared with all of these details so you don't have to think about them in your limited morning time.

2. **Get to bed earlier.** It seems obvious, but this can be very difficult if you're a natural night owl. Some people just function better in the evenings, and unfortunately the 9-to-5 workday doesn't accommodate this. Some workplaces are more and more incorporating the idea of flextime (come in earlier or later, as you please), but if you're not in one of these situations, you'll have to make do with the schedule you're given. Rather than going to bed an hour earlier and lying there wide awake, you might need to ease yourself into it. Try having the lights out a few minutes earlier every night for a few weeks and see if you can train yourself into getting to sleep at an earlier time. Don't rely on prescription medication, alcohol, or other substances, though. These will either leave you feeling groggy in the morning, or may (in the case of alcohol) act as a stimulant and wake you up later.

3. **Get up at the best time for you (within reason).** You may have seen motivational speakers and life coaches talk about how they get up at 5:00 a.m., and how it's glorious, because they have time to meditate for an hour, relax in their personal hot tub, and reflect on life, the universe, and everything in the stillness of the morning. For those of us living in the real world, none of this is going to be very good advice. If you know that getting up at 6:00 a.m. will simply not work for you, and that you can function better getting up at 6:45 a.m., then do that. Don't be bullied into what you "should" do because an overly chipper morning person tells you to. Listen to your body, and get up when it feels best, allowing for the time you need. Try getting up ten minutes earlier than you absolutely need to, and see how that works for you.

4. **Use a second alarm not near you.** There are many kinds of alarms out there, and your phone undoubtedly has one. Try not to use something that shocks you awake; these can actually be bad for your heart and your system over time. If you know that you need extra time just to wake up, build that into your

alarm routine. A great way of forcing yourself to get up, if you need it, is to place a second alarm at the other side of your bedroom, or even out in the hall. It's far too easy to press the "snooze" button on your bedside alarm or phone and just drift off to sleep again, but if you have to actually get out of bed to go turn off the other one, you'll be far more likely to stay up and get on with it. Yes, you might be annoyed, but you'll be up!

5. **Don't make important decisions.** If you have any key decisions to make for work projects, don't leave them until morning, which is basically the last minute. You might feel like you need to sleep on something, but if you're left with a small amount of time to weigh it over again in the morning, you might not be exercising your best judgment. You might be uncertain as to what to do the night before; in that case, at least try to write down a few options then, so that you'll have narrowed down your choices for the morning.

6. **Create a routine.** Make an order for what you do and when you do it each morning, and stick to it. Don't eat breakfast first one day, then shower first the next, and so on. Create a schedule (allowing for the occasional unexpected change-up): "Shower at 7:00 a.m., breakfast at 7:20," and so on. Again, do whatever works for you. You may have to try it out several times before you hit on the combination that works best for your mornings. The more you get used to a routine, the easier it will be to follow.

7. **Make breakfast easy.** Preparing an elaborate breakfast every morning is probably not going to be an option. If you like to cook, try making meals ahead of time on Sundays that you can heat up quickly. Otherwise, instant oatmeal, quality cereal, fruit, yogurt, toast/bagels, etc., are all good options. Don't skip

breakfast, or you will likely be cranky and even light-headed later on. If you can't survive without your morning coffee first, make that a priority; do whatever you need to get going. But do take the time to eat something.

8. Be flexible. Not every morning will go as planned. Maybe you need to be in at work a half hour earlier on some days. Maybe bad weather is making the commute hellish. Always try to know what you'll need in the mornings before you have to confront it, and you'll be far less stressed getting yourself out the door. Check things like the weather and traffic before leaving, just to get a sense of what's going on (see the next section, "Seven Suggestions for Planning Your Commute").

A lot of people simply aren't morning people and never will be, but with a bit of planning, you can make your limited morning time less of a hassle and make it work better for you.

> **"Lost wealth may be replaced by industry, lost knowledge by study, lost health by temperance or medicine, but lost time is gone forever."**
>
> **—SAMUEL SMILES**

SEVEN SUGGESTIONS FOR PLANNING YOUR COMMUTE

Unless you have the option of working from home (see "Is Working from Home for You?" on page 63), you're most likely going to have some kind of commute to your workplace. This can be anything from relatively easy to a huge pain, depending on your location and your workplace location. Since this will be a big part of your job, you need to do some serious thinking on how you'll go about it before you even take the job.

1. **Factor in your commute time when deciding on taking a job.** Obviously, it will probably be too late for this for many readers, but if you are considering working some place in particular or have had a job offer from a company you like, you need to consider how long the commute will be and how it will affect you. An hour each way might not seem bad, especially if you're young and full of energy, but it might become a real drag six months in, or when the days get dark and the snow starts falling. Ask about commute options during your interview, and see if your potential job has, for example, dedicated parking for employees or a shuttle service.

2. **Beware of commutes that are too long.**
Again, if you are in the position of job-searching or accepting an offer, be careful in making your choice if the workplace is far away. Numerous studies in Europe, Australia, and the United States have shown that the longer the commute, the greater its negative effect on productivity and job satisfaction. The commuters surveyed regularly responded that commuting

was the most negative thing about their mornings. Those with longer commutes reported more unplanned absences from work than those with shorter ones. Clearly, a higher salary won't necessarily compensate for your loss of time, and you may find yourself feeling resentful if you're stuck in a particularly long commute every day, even if you like your job and its benefits.

3. **Decide how you will get there.** You'll need to figure out if you'll be driving or taking public transit. Both of these options will have its own costs and complications. Public transportation might take a bit longer, but it might be cheaper than driving and spare your car a lot of wear and tear, or spare you the aggravation of looking for parking each morning. On the other hand, if you have to walk several blocks to a bus or train, either from your home or from your office, you may be concerned about personal safety in the evenings. Studies have shown that, in general, commuting by car is far more stressful, even though you have more control over your trip. Again, various studies have shown that those who find some other way to commute feel more energized at work and are able to perform better on the job.

4. **Practice your commute before talking a job.** Try it out as if you were going to the office: at the same time, from the same location, etc. Try it in the morning and the evening if you can. Try driving, try public transit, and see how it all works and feels like to you. This might be the make or break on what your final decision is.

5. **Use your time well on public transit.** You could just put the earbuds in and zone out, and honestly this is entirely acceptable on some mornings. But consider using that time for other things than checking your phone and social media. Commute time can be for obvious things like reading books or listening to podcasts, but maybe it can also be a time to study a language or another educational project you're interested in. Research has shown that using some of this time to ease in to your workday can make the transition less jarring. This doesn't mean that you

need to be starting work before you even get to work (which is a bad idea if you're not being paid for that time), but activities like making a list of the things you need to do for the day or even over the course of the week can get you ready to face them at work, and maybe even spend less time procrastinating. There are numerous apps to let you make lists, make notes, prepare for meetings, and other activities.

6. **Be efficient if you have to drive.** If you're stuck behind the wheel, you're obviously not going to be able to read or check your phone, though the number of people who do look at their phones while driving is alarming. **Please** don't do this! Instead, you can make use of that time with podcasts and radio. It can be a great chance to carpool. See if a system is already up and running in your area, and if you can join. Or, even if you have a work colleague who lives near you, offer to do alternate driving with them. This will get one more car off the road and provide you with a chance to socialize a bit before work, which has been proven to decrease one's negativity about the whole commuting process. Be sure to keep your car maintained well (brakes, tires, etc.). Also, don't store a lot of things in your car that will weigh it down. This will decrease fuel efficiency and force you to pay for more gas. While you don't want to be checking your phone, having a traffic app installed that can warn you of accidents and slowdowns is essential.

7. **Try alternate ways of commuting.** If your situation allows for it, try out different ways of commuting to see which one suits you. If you drive every day, try out public transportation once in a while to see if it saves or costs you time, or if you feel more productive on the job. You may even be in the enviable position of being able to change up how you commute to your job, to give yourself some variety. If you normally take a bus, is it possible that in warmer months, you might be able to bike to work? Some trains allow for bikes on certain cars, and biking once in a while might provide a great change of scene when the weather permits.

SIX TIPS WHEN MAKING A DAILY SCHEDULE

One great way of saving time is to make a plan for yourself for each day of the workweek. Obviously, you'll already have a good sense of what you're doing, but you might not have allocated enough time for one task over another. If you know how you work, and what the best times of day are for you to do certain things, you'll be able to use your time more efficiently and not feel scattered or overwhelmed. Sticking to a schedule also gives you a sense of stability and routine. Obviously, things will come up and upset the apple cart, and you may get called away to do other things, but having an overall plan will help you manage your time in the long run.

1. **Download a work-schedule template.** There are numerous versions of these online. They are effectively calendars that go in to more detail. You can set out specific tasks by specific dates, keep track of deadlines, and so on. You can store them on your phone or other device and fill them in as needed; with some versions, you can print them out and handwrite in your tasks, if that method works better for you (and there is evidence that the good, old-fashioned way of writing notes and tasks down by hand helps you remember them better). Look around and find a schedule that appeals to you. Some are laid out by the hour, but you can also find schedules that let you mark off tasks by the quarter hour, which can be very useful if you have a lot of small jobs to do.

2. Prioritize your work tasks. Your individual job may well dictate to some extent what you need to do in what order, but many productivity experts recommend getting the most important tasks done first. Putting those at the top of your schedule will ensure that you have enough time to complete them and aren't scrambling at the end of the day.

This can also be done for a weekly schedule, so that come Friday, you're not still facing something that could have been finished midweek. See the next section for more on prioritizing.

3. Use the time-chunking method. This will establish how much attention to give to any one task at a given time (see page 23). Chunking will let you put your best effort into a task without getting burned out on it. If you prioritize an important job, get started on it right away, and are still slogging through it at noon, you're going to feel pretty burned out and may not be of much use in the afternoon. But if you allocate an hour for it, do something else, and then come back to it, say, thirty minutes later, you're more likely to feel that you can handle it.

4. Don't just schedule one thing after another. We all have our own particular flow, and we wax and wane in our energy and productivity throughout the day. You probably already have a sense of whether you're a morning person, an afternoon person, or an evening person. So when you make a schedule, don't

just fill up every available time with a new task; allow a small bit of time in between. If you have a task scheduled for 10:00 a.m. to 10:30 a.m., schedule your next task to begin at 10:35 a.m. or 10:40 a.m. This not only builds in a little extra time in case the work runs over, but it gives you a few minutes to breathe before diving back into the next project. If you know that you hit a slump in midafternoon, try not to schedule a massive project or detailed meeting for that time (and yes, sometimes, you can't avoid those). Listen to your own rhythm, and try to coordinate your day around the times when you'll be able to give your best.

5. **Consider creating a master list of all your tasks.** You can then break this down into monthly, weekly, and daily jobs to get a better sense of the big picture. Maybe you work on one project that's only due once every two weeks, while another task has to be completed twice a day. Seeing it all written down will give you a good sense of where your focus and energy needs to be.

6. **Check out your older schedules to see how you're doing.** Every month (or however long feels right), go back and look over your schedules and see how well they worked for you. Did you use your time efficiently? Did you overschedule? Did you have a lot of downtime? You'll be able to use that information to adjust and fine-tune, so that you can have a schedule and plan that works for you.

> **"Until you value yourself, you will not value your time. Until you value your time, you will not do anything with it."**
>
> **—M. SCOTT PECK**

FIVE IDEAS TO PRIORITIZE YOUR WORK TASKS

Setting down what's most important in your workday is vital to getting control of your work time. Of course, everything will seem important to someone. Your boss may have tasks already prioritized for you, and you'll need to follow those guidelines. But even in this situation, it might be possible to group jobs together to make the best use of your time.

1. **Do what you hate first, if possible.** A quote erroneously attributed to Mark Twain states: "If you have to eat a live frog, it does not pay to sit and look at it for a very long time!" He didn't say it, but it makes sense. In the business world, it's come to mean that if you have something you really don't want to deal with (especially first thing in the morning), the longer you wait to do it, the more difficult it's going to get. You might not be able to cope with getting on with it at 9:00 a.m., but make a point of scheduling it earlier, rather than later. Sometimes, you'll just need to "eat the frog" and get it over with. The upside to this, of course, is that once it's done, it's done, and the rest of the day may not seem as bad.

2. **Assess value.** You may have several tasks that have priority, but it's a good idea to rank them, as much as you're able to. Two things may seem of equal importance, but look for which one needs attention first. External and client tasks often take priority, so if you need to talk with clients on the phone, do that before working on a database problem, unless the two are linked. The more you practice this kind of assessment, the easier it will become.

3. **Use the Eisenhower Decision Matrix.** U.S. president Dwight Eisenhower once demonstrated a way of prioritizing his many tasks and duties by categorizing them in terms of urgency and importance. Basically, urgent tasks need immediate attention (key emails, phone calls, deadlines, etc.), while important tasks (things for the overall business, long-term plans, etc.) might be left until later. Classify each job you have to do as a mixture of both:

- **Urgent and important:** Take care of these first.

- **Urgent but not important:** See if someone else can attend to them while you work on the urgent and important tasks.

- **Important but not urgent:** These can often be left until later in the day or even the week.

- **Not important or urgent:** Try to get out of doing these altogether, if you can.

Again, your boss may make these calls for you, and you may be stuck doing something that doesn't seem urgent at all, but management wants it done right away. If so, you'll just have to get on with it. But if you have some say in how you prioritize tasks, this can be a very good model to follow.

4. Try out the Ivy Lee Method. Ivy Lee was a productivity consultant who lived and worked a century ago. His simple process for prioritizing still works and can be applied to almost any work situation. It's a very straightforward method of getting work done that may or may not work for you, but that many have found very effective over the last century:

- At the end of your day, write down the six most important things you need to do tomorrow. Don't write down more than six.

- List these out in order of importance.

- The next day, work on your first task. Work only on that job until it's completed.

- Then go through the rest or your list in a similar manner.

- Do this each day.

This method is different from chunking (see page 23) or devoting, say, a solid thirty minutes of time to one task before moving on. It may not be for everyone, but for those who do use it, they claim that it helps tremendously with time management and forces them to stay focused until a task is finished. Give it a try and see if it works for you.

5. Be OK with cutting some things from your list. It's highly likely that some tasks will not get done today and can wait until tomorrow. Don't feel defeated about this. If a job is not urgent, let it carry over into the next day, when you'll have more time to attend to it.

EIGHT ACTIONS FOR PRIORITIZING EMAILS

Emails are still a fact of life in the business world. You may have to deal with a lot of them, or very few. But it's almost inevitable that you'll have to deal with some inbox clutter from time to time. If you're feeling overwhelmed and bombarded, here are some suggestions for getting your virtual mail under control.

1. **Set aside specific times to read through your emails.** Don't just go to your work inbox randomly throughout the day; this is a sure way of wasting time. Some studies suggest that it can take more than twenty minutes to really get back into what we were doing before an interruption, and checking your email throughout the day is a definite interruption. Set aside specific times to check emails, say once in the morning and once or twice in the afternoon. Take the time to read though what's there and respond to anything important as needed. But at other times, stay away and focus on your other tasks. Unless you know that you're about to receive an important communication, the inbox can wait until your next scheduled time to check it.

2. **Use the Eisenhower Decision Matrix.** As with tasks (see the previous section), this simple method of categorization will give you a good way to determine what's urgent, important, or not. Classify each of your emails as one of the four categories and deal with them accordingly.

3. Use flagging and starring. Most email programs allow you to classify emails by importance, so get in the habit of doing this for every email. For those of lower priority, you can set them aside in a separate folder (see below) to deal with later.

4. Create subfolders. Try grouping emails by subject, sender, level of importance, etc. After you read and/or respond to an email, file it away in the appropriate subfolder. It will help you keep your inbox clearer and save you time when looking up important emails. Going into your inbox and seeing hundreds of old emails in a long scroll that you haven't filed is a sure way of feeling defeated and overwhelmed.

5. Learn to skim. Depending on how many emails you receive and how long they are, you may need to develop the ability to skim for those of highest importance. Sometimes, you'll receive emails that are flagged by the sender as "high importance." This may be true (but let's be honest, often it isn't!), but don't do this yourself. Everyone thinks their own emails are important. Try to discourage your colleagues from doing this. If you're receiving a dozen emails a day all flagged as "important," how will you know which to respond to first?

6. Reply only to the emails that can be done quickly. If you can respond and take care of something in two minutes or less, go for it. But if it's going to take a longer, more thought-out response, leave it for the moment.

7. Don't feel the need to respond to everything. Some emails require your immediate attention, but a lot of them can be left until a later time or not answered at all. It's best not to get into email "conversations" that can take up your time (go and speak to them in person instead; it will save a lot of time!). So don't feel obligated to respond to everything you receive, unless there is a valid reason. If an email needs an answer but not right away, put it in a special "To respond later" folder, and get back to it when you have time.

8. **Keep your inbox free of spam and nonwork emails.** It should be obvious, but keep your work email as spam-free as possible and don't start accepting emails that are personal in nature. This includes signing up for newsletters not related to work, and similar emails. Keep your work inbox as clear as possible!

> **"One worthwhile task carried to a successful conclusion is worth half-a-hundred half-finished tasks."**
>
> **—MALCOLM S. FORBES**

SEVEN TIPS FOR EFFICIENT WORK ORGANIZATION

> Organizing your daily schedule is essential, and as we've seen, having a plan going in will make you feel better about how you approach your day. No two workdays will be exactly alike, but there are some steps you can take on your side to make days more productive and ensure the best use of your time.

1. **Again, ditch multitasking.** Resist the temptation to juggle multiple projects at once. It just doesn't work, and will only leave you feeling tired, confused, and frustrated.

2. **Commit to your schedule.** If you've made a daily schedule (see page 37), be sure to actually stick as close to it as possible. Of course, sometimes things come along and mess up your plans, but try to keep to the times you've allotted for everything.

3. **Keep your workspace clear.** A cluttered working environment leads to cluttered thoughts and disorganization. Have only what you need where you need it. Don't let paper pile up, and don't let unrelated documents share the same space. If you have a filing system at work, make use of it. When something is no longer needed, file it away, recycle, or shred it, based on company policy. Don't let pens, pencils, and notepads sprawl all over your desk. Keep everything organized in one, neat place. The psychological effect of having a clean and organized work area will make you feel more relaxed and less scatterbrained.

4. Make notes. One area where you can (temporarily) ignore the advice not to clutter is to make notes for yourself of work items that need your immediate attention: reminders, to-dos, phone numbers, etc. You may want to enter all of these on your phone or tablet, but even good old-fashioned post-it notes are great because you see them and they constantly remind you what you need to do next. Just be sure to clear them out when the task is done!

5. Try to be ahead of schedule. If you have a deadline for a project to be in at 4:00 p.m., try getting it done by 3:00, if you can do just as good a job. It never hurts to be early, so long as quality doesn't suffer. Incidentally, this kind of diligence and attention to detail will probably be noticed by your higher-ups, if you're looking to advance your career. And it will give you a bit more time for other things. Of course, some things will occupy you until the last minute, but once in a while, being early is ideal!

6. Watch your own workload. You may want to volunteer to take on extra work or to help out in a crunch. While this can be commendable, you need to be careful about overextending yourself. Likewise, if you are starting to get assigned too much work and can't complete needed tasks by the end of the day, it's going to hurt you in the long run, to say nothing of wasting your valuable time. You may need to talk to your boss about your workload and see if tasks can be spread around a bit more. Likewise, don't assume that you're the only person capable of doing the job. Unless it's a highly specialized task, that's probably not true. It's OK to take a step back and let someone else do it once in a while, especially if it saves you time. Delegating jobs can make everyone's life easier. See page 55 for more.

7. Ask if meeting times can be reduced.

Many meetings are long, boring, and let's be real, unnecessary. The amount of time wasted in them is astonishing. Sure, there are things that require meetings and group attention, but they can also be one of the biggest wastes of time in the office. Even making a commitment to trimming ten or fifteen minutes off each meeting will probably save every attendee several hours a month that could be better spent. Try approaching your boss with that math and see if it gets results! See page 60 for more on making meetings more efficient.

> **"Nothing has ever existed except this moment. That's all there is. That's all we are. Yet most human beings spend 50 to 90 percent or more of their time in their imagination, living in fantasy. We think about what has happened to us, what might have happened, how we feel about it, how we should be different, how others should be different, how it's all a shame, and on and on."**
>
> **—JOKO BECK**

SEVEN WAYS TO SET REALISTIC GOALS THAT YOU CAN ACTUALLY MEET

We may start the week with good intentions. This is going to be the week that we do [insert ambitious projects here]. We may even write it down, so it has to happen now, right? Right? Unfortunately, no. Your work goals will probably be a combination of things you've been assigned and other tasks that you would like to do that would help you along in your career. If you feel like you're falling behind, even with lists and schedules, here are some suggestions.

1. **Be more self-aware:** What is it about this goal that needs to be done? Why do you want to do it? Why do you need to do it? What will happen if it's done on time? What will happen if it's **not** done on time? Why do you care about it? If you're being assigned work, you obviously will approach your tasks from a different angle, but even here, if you like your job and are concerned about the long-term situation for yourself and your company, you should ask these same kinds of questions. What is motivating you to do this?

2. **Be specific:** Make sure that you define what the goal is and what work you need to do to accomplish it. Be as detailed as you can about the process. If you just write down "get it done by Thursday," that's going to be no help when Wednesday rolls around and you've barely started! Estimate what needs to be done when and create a timetable for yourself, so you can monitor your progress. You'll probably

be breaking the bigger tasks up into smaller parts (and if not, you should!), so map out what can be done each day until the job is finished.

3. Be realistic: Now it's time to assess just what can be done in the time frame you have. Can you do all the work necessary in order to complete the task on time? Or are you going to need help? Do you even have enough time to get it done? One of the key aspects of time management is making sure that you actually have time to do things, so overcommitting yourself to projects you can't realistically finish is only going to be frustrating. If you've been assigned something that you know you can't complete on your own in the time given, don't hesitate to ask for help, either from your coworkers or your boss. Your dedication to getting the job done on time is more important than trying to shoulder the whole thing yourself. You're not Atlas, so don't act like it.

4. Be regular: Work on your projects and goals with regularity. Doing a little on Monday and then leaving it until Wednesday (unless you get pulled away by something beyond your control) is just going to leave you feeling frustrated and swamped, when you realize that you should have given it some attention on Tuesday as well. Make a commitment to doing the needed work every day that you have to work on the project and don't deviate from that, unless it's absolutely necessary. You've created your schedule or plan, so stay with it!

5. Be able to measure your goals: You need to be able to measure your progress as you go along, or you're at risk of getting lost along the way. This goes hand in hand with mapping out the project and the work/time needed each day to get it done. Plus, setting yourself mini-goals along the way will help with morale and enthusiasm. Checking off tasks on a list is a great way to track your progress and make sure you're on track. Seeing that you're now 70 percent done with a project will give you a boost. Think of it like you're writing a report that needs to be 1,500 words long, so you keep monitoring your word count. At 1,000 words, you're feeling good. At 1,400 words, you're feeling great! If you have no idea where you are, you'll feel lost, or could easily go over. Doing too much on a project is as bad as doing too little.

6. **Be willing to modify:** Unexpected stuff happens and suddenly, you're not on track anymore. Or maybe your deadline gets moved up a day or two (hooray), because that's no problem, right? Into every life a little chaos must fall, so be prepared for things to go awry and the need to work around new problems. Try to stick to your original outline as much as possible, but consider budgeting in a little extra time from the beginning to ensure that you can still get it done. Don't make your plan so rigid and time-stamped that it can't allow for any extra minutes or hours of work.

7. **Be willing to check in:** If you've made a weekly planner, go back to it at the end of the week and see how you did? Good? Average? Awful? The first few times you map out your longer-term goals and tasks, you may find that you're way off when the end of the period comes, but you'll get the hang of it with practice. Look back at your list or plan. What did you finish? What didn't get done? Why not? If you have regular weekly tasks, did you allow enough time to do them, or even too much? You'll be able to fine-tune your plans as you go along, which will make setting and meeting goals much easier in the long run. Oh, and all of this work up front will save you valuable time later on!

> # "A year from now you will wish you had started today."
>
> **—KAREN LAMB**

BREAKING DOWN BIG JOBS TO SMALLER, MANAGEABLE ONES

At work, you'll have small jobs, bigger jobs, and really big jobs. You may be part of a team that is working on a large project that rolls out in two months' time. There will likely be very specific schedules about what's due when and who's doing what. In situations like this, you may not have to do too much of the planning; someone else may have already done the heavy lifting of determining what needs to be done at what time and how much time the whole project will take. Whether those predictions are accurate or not is an entirely different matter, of course! For your own work, you can use similar strategies. If you're wondering how to best break a big task down into smaller task, here are some tips.

- **Understand the big picture.** What's the end result? What's the desired outcome? Without an understanding of what you're supposed to do, you won't get very far. This may seem like stating the obvious, but if there isn't a clear reason why, it will be easy to get off track in the middle of the project. If you're unsure of the goal, ask.

- **Understand tasks versus projects.** Though they can be used interchangeably, a "task" in the business world is often used to define something that can be done in one go, whereas a "project" is more often something that is spread out over days, weeks, even months. A project may be composed of many tasks, of course. At the same time, a task might be big in its own way, and take up your entire day or leak into the next one. Decide if you have a task or a project.

- **Understand the time frame.** You need to know when the project absolutely must be finished. Working back from that, you can get a sense of what needs to be finished by when. This should be a given, but sometimes projects are left open-ended, which can be confusing and lead to delays. Always try to get the deadline as soon as possible. If there isn't one, maybe consider asking nicely (i.e., pressuring someone!) for one?

- **Look at ways to break down the project.** This might be by time: certain parts must be completed by certain dates, even if you only have a week to get it done. Or it might be divided up by work category or even the type of work to be done. If you've not been given direction on this, look for ways that you can divide the project up that seem logical to you. The goal is to take a big thing and make it smaller.

- **Set specific smaller goals.** Once you have a sense of how to divide up the bigger job, set specific goals for how each portion will be completed: what needs to be done and by what date. Studies show that we work better with a series of smaller and more specific goals. Also, by setting and meeting smaller goals, we get a little dopamine rush, a self-pat on the back for a job well done, which can help spur us onward to completing the bigger project. "Get this white paper written by Friday" is vague and too general. "Write five pages each day from Monday to Wednesday, and add in sources and edit the whole thing on Thursday" is a much more detailed and realistic plan. You just have to force yourself to abide by it!

- **Solicit feedback.** You will probably already be getting some from your boss or the project manager, but it's important to know where you stand. If you're working more independently on a project, have a coworker or other colleague weigh in and tell you how it seems to be progressing from the outside. Don't be afraid of what you'll hear; studies have shown that even negative feedback can be motivating (as long as it's not devastating!).

> "Time is the coin of your life. It is the only coin you have, and only you can determine how it will be spent. Be careful lest you let other people spend it for you."
>
> —*CARL SANDBURG*

DELEGATING AND SHARING WORK TASKS

Sometimes, it's just not possible to go it alone. If you want to take back control of your time, you have to remember that you only have so much of it in any given workday. It's possible that sometimes you'll be overloaded with work; maybe your boss thinks you can handle more than you can, or maybe you got overeager and volunteered to take on extra (hey, it happens!). But it's certain that sometimes, you'll need to delegate and share. This might seem quite easy, but people get wrapped up in their work and projects, and it can be hard for them to let go. If you're especially attached to your own way of doing something, you may be convinced that it's the best (i.e., the only) way to do it, and having to hand that off to someone else can be difficult, no matter how overworked you are. Here are some ideas about sharing and spreading the love, er, work around a little more, so that you can get back some of your own time.

- **It may not be up to you.** You may think that you're on top of it all, but your boss may see it differently. If you're working hard but falling behind, someone higher-up might make the call that you need to share the workload. If this happens, you can either argue against it (probably a waste of time), or accept it gracefully. If it's a very specific task for which you're uniquely qualified, you might have a case to make to oversee the project, while accepting assistance from someone else. Again, be realistic about what you can do. Sometimes others see our situation more clearly than we do.

- **If you're the boss, lose the idea that only you can do the job.** Delegating is one of the chief responsibilities of a good manager. If you have employees or a great team on hand, remember that they were hired for their expertise, so get comfortable with the idea of delegating. Delegation is not just shoving your own work off on someone else; it's realistically spreading around work to get the project done in a timely and efficient manner.

- **If you're an employee, it's OK to ask for help.** You may or may not have the authority to give some of your work to someone else, but it's certainly fine to ask colleagues and your boss for assistance when you're in too deep. In fact, reaching out to a coworker can be a great way to bounce around new ideas and see if you can be more efficient together. And don't hesitate to offer your own help in return. Being there to help the others in your office is a great way to ensure that they are making the most of their time, too. Asking your boss for some help in finishing a job (he or she may delegate some of the work to others) is not a sign of failure or weakness. It actually shows that you are invested in making sure that it gets done properly.

- **Accept that maybe someone else can do it better.** If you've been assigned something that's just not a good match, it might be that there is another person in your office or workplace who could do it better. Of course, we want to look good and impress our managers, but if you're just not able to do the work properly, it's fine to be a bit humble about it. First you have to admit that to yourself, and that's not always easy! If someone else could finish the job in less time, see if you can work on it together, with that person taking over as the lead. It's likely that at some point, you'll be the expert whom someone else is turning to for help!

- **When a task goes from solo to shared, it's OK to check up on it.** If you've needed to offload some of your work to another or several others, it's fine to check in with them and see how it's going, especially if you're the recognized expert on the subject. If you find yourself constantly worrying that the whole thing is going to get messed up, you'll probably need to learn to let go a little bit more. But having a reasonable skepticism is just fine. You want to make sure that anything you started gets finished properly and on time.

> **"The most efficient way to live reasonably is every morning to make a plan of one's day and every night to examine the results obtained."**
>
> **—ALEXIS CARREL**

SIX WAYS OF ADDING VARIETY TO YOUR WORK

Let's face it, no matter how much you enjoy your job, there are going to be days, weeks, whenever that are a slog and just plain boring. Sometimes, you'll just have to accept this as the trade-off for an otherwise good job and a paycheck. But if you find yourself getting bored at work on a regular basis, you'll fall into wasting time and losing productivity, as well as losing enthusiasm. You may not have the most exciting job in the world, but here are some steps you can take to add a little variety and help keep your interest when things get dull.

1. **Review your own tasks.** Take a good look at everything you need to do over the course of the day. If you've created a daily schedule, you'll know by now what you need to do and about how long it  takes to finish each task (unexpected interruptions notwithstanding). You may have a plan to get the most difficult tasks done early, which can be great for budgeting your time, but if you're left with a bunch of tedious things to tend to as the afternoon wears on, you may get bored and start wasting time anyway. Is there something boring but easy and quick you could slot into a fifteen-minute morning routine? This will save you a little time on the other end.

2. **Talk with your boss or supervisor.** Reach out to your boss and let them know that you're feeling a bit underwhelmed by your work. Showing that you have the initiative to get out of the rut and contribute more will make you look great. Ask if there are any solutions and see what other tasks might be more interesting to you.

3. **Ask for something more challenging.** If you are feeling stuck doing repetitive work that doesn't challenge you and isn't a good use of your talents, try approaching your manager or supervisor about the possibility of working on something less easy. Maybe your boss has been reluctant to assign you something else because you show an aptitude for your current tasks and are good at getting them done on time. Go over any options with them and see if anything appeals to you. But be careful about asking for something new to do just for the sake of it being different. You may find that you are not suited to it, it's not in your skill set, or, even worse, it's just as boring as the task you're trying to leave behind!

4. **Ask if you can share around the boring work.** Boring tasks are an inevitable part of most workplaces. And you'll get stuck with having to do some of them. But consider asking your boss and coworkers if it's possible to spread the boredom around a little more, if you and others feel that you might have more than your share. Find out how your coworkers are handling their tasks. They may be bored, too, but afraid to speak up.

5. **Try gamifying some of your work.** Gamification is all the rage these days, and is simply the process of using game psychology to improve working conditions and make tedious tasks more fun. Various studies have shown impressive increases in productivity when some of these principles are applied to work tasks. Research the topic and see if it's for you. There are countless apps out there that let you set challenges for yourself based on the tasks you need to complete. You can try to earn rewards and points, and generally make your boring experiences a little more enjoyable. Treating your tasks like game challenges might be the perfect strategy for you!

6. **Take quick breaks.** You're no good to anyone if you're feeling zonked and zombielike over doing repetitive tasks. And the longer you do them, the more you're going to feel like you're in a fog. It's good, even essential, to get up and stretch periodically, take a quick minute-long walk, and clear your head. These kinds of micro-breaks can be very good for clearing your head enough to get back to the job.

SEVEN WAYS TO MAKE MEETINGS MORE EFFICIENT

Meetings have a bad reputation as classic time-wasters. While sometimes (not all the time), they are necessary, they also tend to go on too long, and everyone looks checked out or bored to tears by the end of them. If meetings are getting out of hand in your workplace, talk to your boss and your coworkers about streamlining them and making them more efficient. And if you regularly have to attend meetings or, even worse, are asked to organize them, here are some tips for how to make them more efficient and keep from wasting your time and everyone else's.

1. **Ask if the meeting is really necessary.** It may seem silly, but a lot of meetings simply aren't needed. There is a kind of meeting culture in modern workplaces, where it feels like more is getting done by meeting, but often these subjects could be done through work chat, email, or smaller, even one-on-one meetings. If the number of big meetings in your workplace seems to be too many or is creeping up, talk with your coworkers and boss, using the idea that these are infringing on work time as a good starting point.

2. **Be prepared.** Whether you're the organizer or attendee, bring everything you need and be ready to go. Don't be fumbling through your notes or have to leave the meeting to get something from your desk. The

point is to get through this as quickly and efficiently as possible. Respect your coworkers' time and come in prepared.

3. **Ask for an agenda.** The meeting needs to be structured and limited to only a few topics. The more focused it can be, the more people will feel engaged. A long-winded meeting that tries to cover everything imaginable will not only waste people's time; they'll start checking out halfway through, and it won't even serve its purpose. As with projects, break meetings down into smaller components, with smaller, mini-meetings replacing big gatherings.

4. **Ask that meetings start and stop on time.** This is entirely reasonable. It's extremely annoying when you show up on time, and everyone else—including the organizer—just saunters in five or more minutes later. It's disrespectful and wastes time. The same holds for the end of a meeting. People are probably already getting agitated to leave, so if you're presenting, don't make them stay any longer than promised, and, if attending, don't waste everyone's time with comments or questions that aren't directly relevant to the topic at hand. Any other subjects can be discussed in private later on.

5. **Ask that only those who really need to be there are invited.** How many times have you had to attend a meeting that you really didn't need to be at? How did you feel about that? Exactly! It may be that your meetings will be more focused and get more done if they only include the key people. If that means the meeting is with three people, so be it. It will save time for the nonessentials. Someone who doesn't absolutely need to be at this particular meeting might be essential at the next one.

6. Discuss the important topics right from the beginning.
This serves several purposes. Primarily, it allows everyone to get right into whatever it is you're there for, which will keep people more engaged, especially if you're brainstorming or trying to solve problems. But it also allows for some people to leave if they have contributed everything they can to that portion of the meeting. Letting people get back to their own work as quickly as possible is a great way to make everyone's time more useful.

7. Ask for minutes, notes, or a summary. Instead of going over everything again at the end of the meeting, ask that there be a good written summary of all the issues discussed. This can come from the organizer's notes or whatever is a good source. This summary can then be emailed to everyone who attended, and they can review it in their own time.

**"To do two things at once
is to do neither."**

—PUBLIUS SYRUS

IS WORKING FROM HOME FOR YOU?

The idea of working from home is probably very appealing if you've never done it before: sleeping in later, no commute, lounging in comfortable clothes, working on your couch or even in bed, taking a nice two-hour lunch in the middle of the day, working until midnight because that's when you do your best work . . . it all sounds marvelous! But working from home brings its own share of problems, too. People who aren't used to it can get bored, miss human interaction, or find it difficult to stay motivated. If you have the chance to work from home one or more days a week, or maybe even full-time, here are some questions to ask yourself and points to remember.

SOME QUESTIONS

- **Can you be alone for long periods of time?** Working from home may seem like a dream come true, especially if you're an introvert. The idea of no distractions, no office gossip, or no other people can be very appealing. But if you are more on the extroverted side, you may find this difficult and frustrating. If you do well in the company of others, then working on your own may seem isolating and counterproductive. You'll need to ask yourself what kind of person you are and whether this work arrangement will work for you more than just occasionally.

- **Can you avoid distractions?** Just because you're at home doesn't mean that there won't be plenty of distractions around you. It's tempting to put on the radio, the television, or your favorite music all because no one is telling you that you can't. You may be able to work just fine like this, but if you know that you're going to have your attention diverted every two minutes by something in the background, you need to be able to discipline yourself to leave it off. This also includes checking your phone and social media.

- **Are you self-motivated?** The idea of home working sounds appealing, but are you capable of getting up and doing it every day? Or even a few days a week? Is there going to be too much temptation to stay in bed until noon and neglect to get on with things until later in the day? Do you need the motivation of getting up and going somewhere to work, or can you provide that motivation yourself?

- **Can you create your own structure?** Without a boss checking up on you regularly, ask yourself if you can be your own boss. You'll need to make your own schedule and commit to it. Of course, you may have tasks given to you that need to be done by the end of the day or the week, but does that mean you'll actually get them done on time? Can you plan out your own week to make sure that everything that needs to get done actually does?

- **Can you communicate?** You won't be able to pop over to the next desk to ask a question. Do you know whom at your workplace you can contact if you need help? Is your manager available? Do they have a preferred method of contact? Can you craft emails efficiently to get all the information you need in one go without having to go back and forth, which will waste your time as you wait for additional answers?

SOME SUGGESTIONS

- **Have a dedicated workspace.** Just as you would at work, it can be very helpful to have a desk to work at. You'll feel more professional if you emulate an office workspace to some extent. You're still going to work, so the idea is to get yourself in that mindset. It's usually a good idea also to get dressed for work, at least in some form. You don't need to put on business attire to sit in your living room or home office (unless you really want to!), but just lounging around in a robe or sleeping clothes all day might make you feel less in the mood to do work.

- **Consider not working at home.** If sitting at home isn't for you, then maybe your "work from home" can be somewhere else: a shared workspace, a café, outside, somewhere where you will feel inspired. It might be that you'll start your day at your desk and end up somewhere else in the afternoon. If this improves your motivation, go for it! If you need more human contact, this can be a great way to telecommute and still have people around.

- **Know your best times for work.** When working at home, you may have more flexibility in when you do things. Maybe your mind is really clear from 7:00 p.m. until 10:00 p.m., and you like to get things done then. This can be great, because it allows you a freedom that conventional office hours don't. If you're going to be home on a regular basis, try experimenting with different times to see if you are more productive during some than others.

- **Take breaks.** Even at home, you can get completely wrapped up in your work, so don't forget to know when to quit for a while. Get up once an hour, walk around, stretch, have a snack, take five minutes to reset. And don't forget to eat breakfast before you start, or eat lunch in the middle of the day!

- **Know when to quit.** Just as it might be tempting to work less when you're at home, it might also be tempting to work more, because you're already home, so why not add an extra hour or two in? This might be fine when you're working on a big project with deadlines looming, but don't get in the habit of it. If you're keeping a fairly regular workday, then finish up at, say, 5:30 p.m. and really be done. If you like working at night, don't put in two or three extra hours in the morning just because you can. Unless you're getting overtime pay, or have a major crunch to get through, say no to the extra hours. Eight hours of work at home is quite enough. See the next section for more on this topic.

One of the key points about owning your time is remembering not to use up too much of it at work. You owe your company your time for the hours agreed on. Typically, this is eight work hours per day. Sometimes you'll get caught up in big projects that require everyone going the extra mile; you might even be eligible for overtime for any extra work, which is always a nice thing! But be careful about accepting or even volunteering for more hours or extra work if you are not being properly compensated. There are provincial and federal laws about the number of hours employees can work, and no company contract or agreement can contravene those. Here are some thoughts about extra work and taking on overtime.

- **Remember that leaving work on time is as important as arriving on time.** You don't want to be the first one out the door when 4:59 p.m. and 54 seconds rolls around (especially if you're new to the job!), but neither do you want to be there at 6:23 p.m., alone in the office, still working on things that everyone else has left until tomorrow. If you're really caught up in something and want to finish it, that's fine once in a while, but don't make a habit of lingering in the office for an extra half hour or more every night. You're allowed and expected to go home at the same time as everyone else, under the terms of your work agreement.

- **Think it over before agreeing to additional work, if you can.** If the extra work or overtime is optional, be sure to think it over properly before saying yes. Ask if you can take a bit of time to make your decision. Be careful about telling yourself that you should do it or that it will help your career. It may, but there are many other factors to consider as well. Are you being asked to stay an extra hour every night? Come on for half a day every Saturday? These kinds of arrangements may not fit in at all with your other responsibilities, so weigh the pros and cons carefully. Never let your boss or anyone else guilt-trip you into more work. You have to know your own boundaries and level of tolerance. If the rest of your life simply doesn't allow for extra work right now, it's fine to decline. You may worry that saying no will reflect badly on you and/or hurt your career, but one incident probably won't have any effect, especially if you have genuine reasons for declining. And if your company would punish you for saying no to being overloaded with work, it may be time to look for another job that is more employee-friendly.

- **Ask your coworkers how they're feeling.** Maybe several of you have been offered more work. Try checking in with them and take the temperature about the whole thing. If everyone is on board, it may be that you'll want to be, too, but again, don't let groupthink influence your decision too much. If several people voice objections for their own reasons, then maybe the whole thing is not such a great idea.

- **Let your boss know if you have any outside commitments that you can't break.** If you have children, are taking night classes, or any other reason, you may not be able to put in extra hours, no matter how much you are needed. Make sure to communicate your needs to your boss as soon as possible. It is illegal for your company to retaliate or punish you for needing pick up your children at a certain time, for example. It might be possible that some compromise can be worked out. Maybe you can put in a few extra hours every Sunday afternoon from home. The point is to be clear about any special conditions from the start.

- **What if you have mandatory overtime?** Your contract may require you to put in extra hours from time to time, especially with deadlines or other urgent matters. This is fine and legal, as long as you are being compensated and other important benefits, such as extra break time, are factored in. These conditions are governed by law, so if you're in doubt, check with your province's employment laws. Working occasional extra hours to get a project across the finish line can leave everyone with a real sense of accomplishment, but make sure that your time is not being abused.

[
"If you would only recognize that life is hard, things would be so much easier for you."

—LOUIS D. BRANDEIS
]

CHAPTER 3:

TIME MANAGEMENT IN YOUR PERSONAL LIFE

Just as it's important to tackle your time at work, it's as important, if not more, to make time work for you during the other 128 (give or take) hours in the week. Being on top of your time in your personal life will make a huge difference regarding how you perform in your professional life, and can also be crucial for your health, mental state, and overall well-being. Studies have shown that relaxation and recreation are essential for you to be able to function. If you're making a commitment to use your work time better, you need to do the same thing for the rest of your life. This chapter explores ways to own your personal time.

NINE WAYS TO MAKE TIME FOR YOURSELF

No one is more important in your life than you. If you're not healthy, not happy, not in control, you won't do your best, and you won't be able to help others. If you're run ragged or feeling frazzled, you can't do things the way you want to and the way they deserve to be done. It's absolutely essential that you get in the habit of making time for yourself. This helps you recharge, get your energy back, clear your head, and get ready to face the next day, week, or whenever. If you're an introvert, you already know the value of alone time, and you probably seek out as much of it as you can. If you're an extrovert, just know that time for yourself doesn't have to mean locking yourself away alone in your home. It means taking time to do things you enjoy, talking time to look after yourself, and being able to get your head back in the game so you can go out into the world ready to take on new challenges. Here are some suggestions for making sure you pay attention to yourself.

1. **Ask yourself what it is that you're missing out on.** You want more time to do things you enjoy, so write down what it is you'd like that time for. You can go a bit wild here; the point is to list the things you would do if you had the time to do them. That can be anything from learning a language, to playing hockey, to gardening, to

building models, to becoming a wine expert. Whatever takes your fancy—
write down the things you want to do, if you only had the time.

2. **Ask yourself what you're currently doing.** Now
make a list of all the things that you're doing in your nonwork time.
This will necessarily include the errands and chores that are a part
of daily life, but add in all the things that you do in your spare time.
You might need to observe yourself over a week or even a month.
Keep a detailed diary or record of what hours you spend doing
what. You'll probably be surprised at how much time you devote to
doing things other than what you want to do, even when you have
the free time to do those things.

3. **Commit to cutting down on unimportant activities.**
Once you can see how much of your free time is being taken up by
nonessential things or at least things that aren't what you really want to be
doing, it's time to make a commitment to cutting down on them. Some
of these will probably be obvious: phone time, social media of all kinds,
computer time in general, streaming television programs and movies, and
all of the digital distractions we've created for ourselves are a major time
suck. That's not to say that you can't do these things, of course; a good
binge-watch with a pizza can be just what you need at the end of a long
week. The point is to see how much of these kinds of activities you're
doing related to how much time you could spend doing things from your
list that you'd really like to do.

4. **Commit to actually doing one of the things you want
to do.** Even if you can only spare fifteen minutes a day, close the
laptop, get off the phone, and make the commitment to actually do one
of those things on your list. Learn a few new words in Spanish, practice
Tai Chi, whatever it is, get on with it! You won't ever get around to it
unless you decide that it's important. And if you have to force yourself to

do it or it starts feeling like drudgery, it might not be something you really want to do.

5. Review your social commitments. We all need friends and interaction. We need people to talk to, laugh with, and share our horror stories from the workweek. Many of us have romantic partners that are at the center of our lives. These connections are all necessary and healthy ways to spend time. But are there social interactions you don't need or that could at least be reduced? Do you have a weekly gathering with work colleagues that you could maybe go to every other week? Did you volunteer for something but got roped into giving it more time than you really intended? Do you have friends who always want to go out on Friday night, even if you're sometimes not in the mood?

6. Learn to say no. It's OK to turn down a social commitment once in a while or to back off on always being available. Sometimes, you just need to put yourself first. We often feel uncomfortable saying no to people because we fear being judged, looking like a wet blanket, or being seen as aloof or antisocial. But saying no is healthy and gives us a chance to reclaim our time and space.

7. Communicate your needs. Tied up with saying no to things, try to develop the idea that it's OK to tell people that you need time to yourself. You don't have to give detailed reasons unless you want to, and you certainly don't have to apologize for it. It should be enough that you have other needs and won't be joining the gang this Friday for a change. If they try to pressure you about it or nag you into giving up your time anyway, you may need to reassess your friendships. True friends should understand. Don't feel guilty about this. Just ask yourself how you would react if a friend of yours canceled something because they needed time alone or any other reason. You'd probably understand, right? Unless they were rude about it? So be OK with telling others what you need.

8. **Organize your home life.** One way to free up your
time is to make sure that everything in your home has a place.
Always keep your keys, your phone, your work material, your
glasses, etc. in the same location so that you can go right
to them whenever you need to. Scrambling around to find
something that you were sure you saw just yesterday can waste time that
adds up. Keep everything you will need for the next day near your door so
that you're less likely to forget it.

9. **Declutter.** Related to keeping everything in its place, make a
commitment to keep your personal space and home free of clutter. This
doesn't have to be about only keeping items that "spark joy." Cleaning
up contributes to psychological well-being. Having piles of papers lying
about in stacks, unwashed dishes, and all of the other things we let go
makes the mind feel messy as well. Committing to keeping these things
tidy on a regular basis costs you a much smaller amount of time than
letting them all pile up and having to devote a whole Sunday to cleaning
once every few weeks. Think about what you could do with that Sunday
instead!

> **"To be able to fill leisure
> intelligently is the last
> product of civilization."**
>
> **—ARNOLD TOYNBEE**

Your work is important, but it shouldn't be more so than those you're close to. If you're spending far too much time at the office, bringing home work, and working late into the night or on weekends, there are two problems: First, you're probably not being paid enough, and you need to nip that in the bud; go ask for a raise or a reduction in your workload. Second, you're neglecting those who matter most and losing precious time with them. And that's the thing that will stay with you in the long run.

Having a network of friends isn't just nice, it's essential for our health. A 2010 study involving a meta-analysis of over 300,000 people across several decades determined that the quality of one's relationships has as much of an effect on our well-being as quitting smoking, adopting a better diet, and taking other health measures do. In fact, people with better social ties have a 50 percent increase in rate of survival over those who don't; that's a stunning statistic! The study authors wrote: "Physicians, health professionals, educators, and the media should now acknowledge that social relationships influence the health outcomes of adults and should take social relationships as seriously as other risk factors that affect mortality."

Sometimes, your work has to come first, but it just can't be all the time. Think about your priorities: How much do your friends, siblings, spouses and partners, and children mean to you? Of course, they mean everything. Very few people say on their deathbed, "I wish I'd spent more time at the office." But they will regret the lost time with loved ones, the putting off saying what should have been said, and dozens of other things that help us bond with others. If you're trying to reclaim some of that important time together with loved ones amid a busy schedule, here are some suggestions.

1. **Take the first step.** If you are really committed to getting more time in with loved ones, take the initiative and reach out, even if it's to people you haven't talked to in a while. You'll probably be surprised at how often others are delighted to hear from you. Send emails and texts, make phone calls, do whatever you need to do to open those lines of communication. Nothing will happen unless someone makes the first move, so don't sit around waiting for others to contact you.

2. **Make get-togethers low-key and easy.** Planning time with loved ones and friends doesn't have to be elaborate and expensive. It's the company of the others that you want. So instead of making plans to go to some trendy bar or fancy restaurant, plan something that everyone can do easily, such as a short meetup in a local park or  a walk that's nearby. Having a few friends over doesn't have to be a big affair either. Invite people to bring their own snacks and make it as casual as you want it to be. The fewer restrictions you put in the way of yourself and others, the more likely people will be to get together, so that you can spend quality time together in the limited time that you all have to spare.

3. **Make time for someone when you don't have it.** Sometimes, you'll be stuck into work that you can't get away from, or something will be keeping you from your loved ones. If it isn't possible to be with them, take a moment to reach out and say hello. Send them a quick email or text, let them know you're thinking of them, say something nice, and that's it! No need to try to make plans or report on your life. Just offering a simple gesture will make their day, and you'll feel great knowing you've done something nice and thoughtful. This kind of action

can take less than thirty seconds, and is great for maintaining bonds and strengthening relationships.

4. Make commitments and keep them. It's easy to make tentative plans with someone and then break them, but if it's in your calendar and you know that it's coming up, you have no excuse to forget it or get busy with something else. Just as you'd be sure to keep a doctor's appointment, be determined to keep that lunch date with your friends. They're just as important.

5. Work on projects together.

This doesn't mean getting everyone over to paint your house, but suggest, for example, that you all get together on a Sunday to plan the week's work meals and then make them together. This is a great way to have some social time that also accomplishes a necessary task for the coming week. You could do this with laundry, grocery shopping, or anything else. Combine weekend errands and chores with a bit of socializing to take the dreariness out of them and also get some time with friends and family that you might not otherwise get to have.

6. Social multitasking can be an option. Multitasking at work is not a good idea, but if you're pressed for time, you might be able to squeeze in some social time while you're doing something else. If you're going through old stacks of papers, dusting your home, or doing anything that doesn't require your detailed attention, phone up a friend and have a chat at the same time. Maybe you can both arrange ahead of time to get something boring done while catching up! Make it into something fun that you can joke about. The point is to look for ways to connect even when your own time is short.

7. Prioritize. Your time may be limited, but always remember what's most important. Everyone moves in different directions, gets involved with other things, and maybe drifts apart. Children grow up astonishingly fast, and you only get one shot to be there for the important moments in their lives. Missing birthdays and other important landmarks because you have to work is something you **will** regret later on, guaranteed. If your job is constantly pulling you away from precious moments you'd rather be experiencing, it might be worth considering whether this job is a good use of your time. You can always make more money, but once time is gone, it's gone forever.

> **"Friendship improves happiness, and abates misery, by doubling our joy, and dividing our grief."**
>
> **—JOSEPH ADDISON**

SEVEN TIME MANAGEMENT TIPS FOR EVERYDAY CHORES AND ERRANDS

Doing all the regular tasks in life can take up a lot of time: grocery shopping, laundry, errands, cleaning, blech! If you have a 9-to-5 job, taking care of mundane tasks pretty much requires nights (when you're tired) and weekends (when you'd rather be doing other, more fun things). You're probably not going to feel very motivated at either of those times to do the work you know you need to do. Here are some ideas about how to get these chores done in a way that takes less of your time and leaves you with more free time to do the important things that matter to you.

1. **Use the chunking method.** Grouping your errands together by location is a great way to check them off a lot faster (see page 25). Don't make extra trips when you can get everything done in one outing!

2. **Try to avoid busy times.** Sure, easier said than done! If you're working a 9-to-5 job, you probably have the option of either evenings or weekends to do many things, both of which can be inconvenient, even if necessary. For grocery shopping, try to go either later in the evening on a weeknight (not a Friday night) or make the effort to get up early on Sunday to be there when the store opens—yes, that's painful! But when you zip in and out in minutes rather than waiting in long lines, you'll be grateful! For other services (anything from dry cleaning to a pharmacy),

try locating ones that are near your workplace so you can zip into them at lunch or just after you leave work. The fewer of these you have to attend to over the weekend, the more time you'll have.

3. **Buy in bulk.** If your budget allows and you have the storage space, buy nonperishable things in larger quantities (such as at wholesale outlets) so that you have to shop for them less often. Having to shop because you've run out of some mundane item can be annoying if it's the only reason you need to go out, and it wastes time.

4. **Keep a cooler and bags in your car.** Why a cooler? So that if you buy refrigerated items at the grocery store, you can put them in there and finish whatever else you need to so without having to rush home. Go buy your groceries at 9:00 a.m., and then you can leave them with confidence in the car and take care of other errands, without needing to go to the supermarket last, when it's more crowded. Try using a basket in your car as well, so that you can bring several bags in at once and not have to make several trips.

5. **Automate and go digital.** Automate your bill payments so that you never have to worry about them. Your work may already be set up for direct deposit of your paychecks. The point is to put all of these kinds of things on autopilot, so that you don't need to spend time in the bank or post office. Look up and download apps that can help make things like grocery lists, to-do lists, and whatever else you might need. Keep a standard shopping list with the main items you buy on your phone so that you don't have to always write up new ones. Apple has "Reminders" preloaded on iOS devices, and it can be a great help in creating lists and literally reminding you of anything you need to do.

Do more of your shopping online to save time, but be mindful that local businesses need your support!

6. Create a space in your home for things you need to do.

Use just a portion of a table or counter, preferably somewhere near your front door. Put anything related to what you need to do there, so that you'll have all of your errands and items in one place. Need to return a library book? Put it there. Need to dry clean a blouse? Fold it up and place it there. You'll be able to see what needs to be done without feeling scatterbrained or worrying about forgetting something.

7. Volunteer to help someone else out with their errands.

Not necessarily a time-saving tip, but if you know someone elderly who could use the help, or maybe a single mother who needs to look after children, why not offer to do some of their errands for them? You can use it as an opportunity to get some of your own tasks done as well, and studies show that helping others is a great way to reduce your own stress and make you feel better. It might even make your own errands feel more rewarding.

HOW TO MAKE THE MOST OF YOUR NIGHTS

> Working a 9-to-5 job means that you don't have much of the weekday to yourself. If you work from home or have alternate hours, your situation may be different, but for purposes of this book, we'll assume that you're doing the typical workday routine. You may be off by 5 or 5:30, but that doesn't mean the end of the day starts. You may have a commute (a long one), you may have family commitments, or maybe you're taking a night class. And you still need to eat at some time! The point here is that you may not even have much of your evening to yourself. So how can you make the most of it? Here are some suggestions.

- **Take time for yourself.** As simple as it seems, allowing some time for yourself is an important first step. Be willing to give yourself that time, and don't just get preoccupied with tomorrow's work, jumping on to social media, or whatever else draws your attention. This can be a surprisingly difficult step for some people to take. Get comfortable with the idea that you deserve some "you" time.

- **Make a change of clothes.** If you're in formal business clothing all day, you'll do this naturally, but if your office is more casual, it may not occur to you to put on anything else. Making the change from working clothes to home clothes, even if they're not substantially different, is a great way to signal a change of scene and get yourself in the psychological state of leaving work behind for the night. Plus, if you *are* wearing business clothes all day, it's going to feel so much better!

- **Drink water.** Before you grab that glass of wine or bottle of beer, take a little time to rehydrate. If you are in a temperature-controlled office all day, it can be dehydrating. It's never a bad idea to drink more water at any time, but this is especially true at the end of the day. Give your body a chance to absorb some extra water before putting any alcohol in you, since that can be even more dehydrating.

- **Make the time to eat.** If you're tired, the temptation may be to snack or grab some junk food, but this won't do you much good in the long run. It's not necessary to prepare a gourmet feast each night (especially if you live alone), but make the effort to eat better, whether that's by pre-preparing meals at the weekends, ordering premade meals from a service, or  even having quality take-out food delivered from time to time. Take a little time to learn how to prepare some simple meals (there are endless recipe sites online). Cooking doesn't have to be complex or exhausting, and you may find that you enjoy the creative process of putting together something. It can be even more fun if you're making food for two. Giving yourself a little time in the kitchen can be a great antidote to the craziness of the day, with the reward at the end that you get to eat what you make!

- **Avoid overstimulation.** It's important to watch what you do in the evenings. It's generally recommended that you not exercise for at least a few hours before going to bed, so if hitting the gym at night is part of your routine, finish up early enough to give yourself a chance to unwind a little. The same goes for stimulants like coffee and alcohol. You may be one of those rare individuals who can slurp down a mug of coffee at 11:00 p.m. and be fast asleep at 11:30, but for most of us mortals, this isn't possible.

Try to cut off your caffeine intake for several hours before going to sleep; some sources recommend as much as six hours. Alcohol can be funny in this regard. If you overindulge, you may feel sleepy an hour later, but the problem is, it may also wake you up at some point after that, so unless you want to be wide awake at 3:00 a.m. after a few late-night glasses of wine, be careful how late you imbibe.

- **Avoid electronic stimulation.** Close the laptop or put away the phone at least an hour before you go to bed. Numerous studies have shown that being glued to a computer screen of any kind can disrupt your sleep. If you're always checking on the latest email, the newest text, or the most recent social media update, it can increase your stress levels. Sometimes work emergencies require you to be connected all night, but try to take some time away if you can, and don't let work intrude too far into your evening.

- **See your nights as a break or a mini-vacation.** Unless you have a major project with an upcoming deadline (which, with luck, won't be too often), consider your evenings to be time away from work (except for what's absolutely necessary). The point is to disconnect and reclaim that time for yourself. Get in the habit of not letting work intrude into your personal time. It's OK to establish boundaries.

- **Be OK with saying no.** It's fine if you just want a night in. You're not obligated to go to every social function and gathering. If you're tired and need some alone time, that's reason enough. If you're feeling obligated to keep up meeting up with others and you're just not in the mood, it's fine to cut back. Your time is limited and you don't need to spend every hour with others.

- **Set aside some time to do the things you want to do.** If you have hobbies, interests, or fun pursuits, give yourself permission to indulge in them. You may not be able to every night, but it's important not to neglect the things that matter to you. Even if you only have a half hour to play your guitar or tend to your bonsai trees, don't let that time go on other things, certainly not just watching television or cruising the internet. Not that there's anything wrong with those activities, if you need a bit of brainless downtime, of course, but don't let them become the only activities that you make time for in the evening. Hobbies can relax and also inspire. Doing something you love may give you insights into how to solve a work problem that's been nagging at you.

- **Unwind before bedtime.** Take some time to be quiet, reflect, and just be. Perhaps you might try some form of meditation or mindfulness. Or it might just be that a good book appeals to you. Some therapists recommend keeping a gratitude journal, a place where you write down all the good things that happened to you during the day. It's nice to be mindful that, even in the midst of stress and bad news, there are almost always good things to be thankful for, little incidents that happen most days. Sending yourself off to sleep in a good mood can be a great way to ensure a better night's sleep and leave you rested enough to face the next day's challenges.

"Everybody's working for the weekend," but having two whole days off isn't always what it's cracked up to be. Everything you've been putting off all week is suddenly staring you in the face: shopping, laundry, cleaning and other household maintenance, family obligations, maybe even a side job . . . all of these can eat up your time so fast that it's Sunday evening before you know it, and you had no time for yourself. If your Saturdays and Sundays are causing you as much stress as the Mondays to Fridays, you'll need to look at how you're using your time, and see if there are better ways to organize your affairs (hint: there are). These tips can help you start reclaiming part of the weekend for you!

- **Take care of Monday concerns on Friday.** If you have a bit of time on Friday afternoon, make the effort to get a start on Monday's tasks. It doesn't have to be something big, but if you can put things into motion then, you'll have a head start on Monday and less to worry about over the weekend. Send those emails, schedule the meetings, read that report, whatever you can do to eliminate the need to work on it over the weekend. Then, it's less to worry about, and you'll have more time for yourself.

- **Make a plan.** It doesn't have to be mapped out down to the most minute detail, but set out a rough weekend schedule for yourself and commit to sticking to it. You'll feel more in control of your time if you know what you want to be doing when. And it's OK to divert from the plan. Spontaneity is important, too.

- **Don't overcommit yourself.** Two whole days off is great, but be careful about overextending yourself, even if you have a relatively free weekend. You don't want to be exhausted by Sunday night and then have to face the workweek. Pick two or three things that you want to do, and limit it to that. There will always be another weekend to try something else. If you're madly booked up from sunrise till well past sunset, you're going to be burned out by Sunday evening.

- **Don't under-commit yourself.** On the other hand, it's OK to once in a while go for it and really enjoy your weekend. If you have something special coming up, make sure that you experience it to the fullest; treat your two days as a mini-vacation and go for it! Life is for living, after all.

- **Get personal work done, but be careful about overdoing it.** If you have a massive list of chores and errands, consider not trying to get everything done in one weekend, unless it's urgent. Maybe you can spread them out over two (or more?) weekends or during weeknights, and make the tasks all seem less monumental. Prioritize whatever needs to be done first and get those things done. If you have the time and energy after that, do a few more tasks, but be willing to let a few nonessential things go until later. If you really don't want to clean the oven on Sunday, leave it until Wednesday night.

- **Do the boring stuff on Saturday, if possible.** If you can, try getting the chores and the tedious things out of the way sooner rather than later. If you can wrap up all those things by early Saturday afternoon, you'll have that much more time for yourself, without having to deal with interruptions at other times throughout the weekend. Don't leave everything until Sunday afternoon, or you'll be very unhappy when it comes around!

- **Make sure to have some downtime.** It's important to recharge, no matter what you're doing over the weekend, even if it's just a list of boring errands. Make sure that you allow yourself a chance to rest, catch your breath, and just be still for a moment, or two, or three. This can be in just about any way that you want it to be: meditation, having a glass of wine, listening to music, bingeing a few episodes of a television show. Make sure that you schedule in some time just for you.

- **Unplug for a while.** The internet and social media will always be there; that's either good news or bad news, depending on your perspective. Your time won't be. So think about how important it is to check those updates or read those texts (probably not very, to be honest). All of that online nonsense will still be around to check later during the week. Let yourself have a bit of time away from it. Make a point of contrasting your weekend time with your weekday time, and it will seem more special.

- **Consider having an occasional day of doing nothing.** We're always convinced that we have to do something to be valuable, but this is a mistake. Our value is not just determined by our productivity. Setting aside a day to do nothing at all can help you refocus and get back in control of your time and your life. Unfortunately, you may not be able to do this too frequently, but once in a while try to give yourself a full day where you do nothing of importance, that is to say, nothing about work, or chores, or any other mundane experience. The idea of a total rest from work is found in some religious traditions and still has much value in the modern world. Taking the occasional opportunity to check out completely can be wonderfully rejuvenating.

- **Make a plan for the week.** If you want to hit the ground running on Monday, spend a little time putting together a plan for your workweek, listing the most important tasks and allocating time for them. Draw up a schedule, if you need to. Just be careful not to obsess over this too much, since plans change, and you don't want to spend long hours of your weekend devoted to planning out the next workweek. Keep it simple, but structured, and you'll feel better when Monday morning rolls around.

- **Avoid the Sunday blues.** We've all had that feeling. The weekend is going great, and then you realize it's 8:00 p.m. on Sunday night, and it dawns on you that the workweek is about to start. Maybe you're not prepared; maybe you needed to have something ready for Monday and haven't done it yet. The best thing you can do is to head this off at the pass before it starts. If you know there is something you need to do before Monday, don't leave it till the last minute. If it's a big task, do a little bit at a time throughout the weekend, to avoid it seeming like a monumental job at the last minute (this is the equivalent of not leaving your college term paper until the night before). Getting the task out of the way leaves open the evening for something more enjoyable. Don't let your Mondays start on Sundays! Consider doing something fun on Sunday evening: a dinner with friends, a movie, a fitness class, or whatever appeals to you. It will give you a last hurrah before the week starts and make the weekend seem longer.

KNOWING WHEN TO TAKE A VACATION

Budgeting your time also means knowing when to take time off, from a few days to a few weeks. Your company will have its own policies about vacation; your weeks may roll over into the next year, or you may have to use them up. However, even if your vacation weeks do roll over, don't just put off taking some time off because you'll get around to it later. Taking regular breaks is essential to help recharge and come back to the job with renewed energy. Understanding when to take a vacation is just as important a part of managing your time as anything else. Here is some advice on how to recognize when it's time to get away for a bit.

- **Work is all you have time for.** If your life is being consumed by work and even your evenings and weekends are not your own, you're in a bad place, and you need to put a stop to it. The sooner you can take a break, the better. You may need to cut yourself off completely in order to reset.

- **Work is constantly irritating you.** There will always be small annoyances at our workplaces, but if you find that everything is getting under your skin lately, it's likely that you need to be away from it for a while to get some perspective.

- **You're making mistakes at work.** Even if you're getting enough sleep and away time, you're still making errors or just not working up to the level that you or anyone else is happy with. This can mean a lack of concentration and commitment, and can be a clear sign that you need a break.

- **You're coping with substances.** If alcohol or other drugs are the only way you can unwind from a vigorous workday, then it's time to look into taking yourself away for a bit. An occasional indulgence won't likely hurt you, but if you need it to cope, then you might have to deal with long-term problems beyond just needing a vacation.

- **Your sleep is suffering.** If you're not getting enough sleep, there can be any number of causes, but if you're fairly sure that it's because you're always thinking and worrying about work, you need to consider removing yourself from the environment for a while for a rest and a reset.

- **You feel stressed all the time.** We all have to cope with a certain amount of stress, but if you're always under pressure and exhibiting physical symptoms (see page 92), you need to take a break.

- **You're dreaming about other places.** It may seem clichéd, but if you find your mind is wandering, if you're fantasizing about the last vacation you took, or if you want to be in a specific place that is decidedly not where you are at the moment, it's a likely sign that you need to get away and actually be in that place you're thinking about!

- **It's been more than a year since your last vacation.** There's nothing noble about sacrificing time off to work. It may seem fine in the short term, but ignoring your needs will eventually bite you on the behind. If it's been a considerable time since your last break, you need to take a look at your life and make the decision to schedule in another vacation.

- **Small rewards and indulgences aren't working.** Sometimes, all we need is a good coffee or a bit of chocolate. A simple reward can be enough to get us back on the proverbial horse and working again with enthusiasm. Or maybe you enjoy some activity on weekends, but it's not bringing you the same joy any more. If you're finding that the little things and brief getaways aren't doing it for you, you need to consider that it's time to go away for a bit.

A vacation doesn't have to mean booking some expensive trip out of the country. Sometimes, just a week at home in your own neighborhood will be enough. But you should consider, if your budget allows, trying to get a change of scene. Even if it's just driving fifty kilometers away to a country hotel or spending a week skiing at your favorite resort in the next province over, the point is to get out of your surroundings and give yourself a chance to experience a fresh perspective. It may not seem like much, but it can do amazing things for your mental and emotional state and leave you much more ready to return to work. Time off is not a luxury—it's a necessity, so make sure you use it!

> If you feel like your time is getting away from you and you no longer have control over your life, you're going to start having negative consequences. Feeling stressed and run ragged is not only bad for your work life; it's bad for your life in general. If your time is just not your own anymore, burnout can follow, both at work and in your personal life and relationships. You may lose your sense of commitment or enthusiasm, and everything will just go downhill from there. Here are some of the signs that you're likely burning out at your job or at life in general, and what you can do to turn things around.

- **Headaches:** Whether tension, migraine, or some other form, headaches are one of the most annoying and miserable things we have to endure. And it's very common for them to increase if you're under stress. If you find yourself reaching for painkillers more and more often, you might want to evaluate what might be causing you extra stress.

- **Muscle tension:** As with headaches, the body tenses up in reaction to stress. This is an evolutionary response that was meant to keep us safe from the very real dangers of prehistoric life. The problem is that when the stress is continual, the tension response never goes away; the body never gets a chance to relax, and the tension becomes chronic.

If your neck and shoulders are always tight, if your legs are cramping up, you might be showing signs of a reaction to outside stressors.

- **Acne:** Stress can cause zits. We all know this. How often has it happened that you were ready for a big night out, a first date, or some other public gathering, and then on the day of the event, a big pimple suddenly made its appearance? It's clichéd enough to be a joke, and yet it's happened to almost everyone. Various studies have shown a connection between higher stress levels and increased acne, even if it's just because we touch our faces more often when stressed. If you find you're breaking out more than usual or if you haven't until now, stress could be a possible cause.

- **Pain:** Pain anywhere in the body can come from numerous sources. But if the pain is chronic, it might be due to muscle and tendon issues, as noted above. The so-called stress hormone, cortisol, has been found in various studies to be higher in people with chronic pain issues such as back pain. This may be a correlation/causation situation, but the fact that both are present indicates that there could well be a connection.

- **Chest pain:** Pain in the chest can be caused by any number of issues, not just heart problems. But if you are experiencing any kind of chest pain, do **not** self-diagnose! Make an appointment to see a qualified health-care professional as soon as possible.

- **Sleep loss:** Insomnia is a classic sign of stress. The next section discusses it in far more detail.

- **Being frequently sick:** Being under stress seems to weaken the immune system. A variety of studies have shown that people who are subject to higher levels of stress are also more susceptible to the flu, head colds, and all the other scourges of the winter months. One study showed that a high-stress control group was afflicted with 70 percent more respiratory infections; that's an astonishingly high number that suggests just how much stress can weaken the body's defenses.

- **Lowered libido:** Sorry to say, but if you're under a lot of stress, your love life may be suffering. Studies have shown that this holds true for women and men, and that high stress levels can have an adverse effect on one's desire and enthusiasm. For men, this can mean erectile dysfunction, and for women and men, a lack of interest.

- **Increased heart rate and blood pressure:** Stress elevates the heart rate in the moment, as we scramble to get out of a dangerous situation. The problem is that a stressed-out person's heart rate can stay in that state if they're being exposed to constant stress. Blood pressure rates can go way up as well. The takeaway is that stress is bad for your cardiovascular system, so if you're finding that your heart seems to be pounding frequently, it could be a sign that you're experiencing too much stress in some area of your life.

- **Digestive issues:** Stress can affect just about everything to do with digestion, leaving you with a loss of appetite, upset stomach when you do eat, heartburn, gas, and other uncomfortable complaints. Weight gain and weight loss are also associated with stress issues. If you're finding eating to be unpleasant and the results even more so, it could be a sign of too much stress in some area of your life.

- **Note:** Please remember that none of this is intended as a substitute for qualified medical care. This section and the next are included as guides to help you look at larger issues that may be affecting you. If you have any of these symptoms, please seek professional medical advice. Your symptoms may be an indication of an underlying condition, but only your doctor will know for sure.

KEEPING AN EYE ON YOUR SLEEP PATTERNS AND MENTAL STATE

One of the key problems with not getting your time under control is, as we've just seen, the stress that comes along with it. You may feel pulled along by your schedule, rather than in control of it. And as shown in the previous section, being stressed can start to have real effects on your physical and mental health. And when those go, nothing else will matter except getting better. Then you won't be good to anyone, not your job, your friends, or your family. Keeping an eye out for warning signs that your health is in danger is something you need to do whenever you're feeling overwhelmed or under too many deadlines. Two areas that are very important in taking care of yourself are the amount of sleep you're getting and your overall mental well-being. Here are some important signs to watch out for and actions to take.

- **You're not getting enough sleep.** This can be one of the biggest challenges when trying to take control of your time: making the time to sleep. Lack of sleep can either be by choice (you're staying up late and getting up early to work on/finish projects), or it can manifest in some form of insomnia. Many people have issues winding down at the end of a day; they can't turn their minds off, their body is tense, or something else prevents them from falling asleep. They may rely on alcohol or other substances to try to help them relax.

On the other side, some people can fall asleep easily enough, but find themselves waking up early, say at 5:00 a.m., and being unable to go back to sleep. This seems to be a prime time either for the mind to start turning over everything you have to do in the coming day, or for people to have worries about what they're doing with their lives and how everything is going to go wrong. If you've experienced either of these sleep issues, don't worry! They affect almost everyone at one time or another. But if you find that either or both are regular occurrences, watch out. Prolonged lack of sleep is not only bad for your work performance; it can do lasting damage to your health.

Studies have shown that lack of sleep can lead to:

- **Memory loss:** Not getting enough sleep can have a detrimental effect on your ability to learn and remember information. If your job requires you to take in a lot of new information, you're going to start falling off pretty quickly. If you're a student, this is even worse.

- **Lack of alertness:** It should be fairly obvious, but not sleeping can leave you feeling groggy and less able to concentrate, exactly what you don't want on the job. Further, this lack of alertness could continue when you're in your car or in other potentially dangerous situations. Being chronically tired greatly increases your risk of having accidents. It's estimated that in the United States, fatigue and lack of sleep accounts for over 100,000 accidents a year. Canada's numbers are proportional.

- **Depressed immune system:** When you sleep, your immune system releases proteins known as cytokines, some of which are needed to fight infections and inflammation. Lack of sleep can lower the number of these proteins, making you more susceptible to infections over time.

- **Risk for other illnesses:** Many studies link a lack of sleep with heart disease, high blood pressure, and diabetes, among other illnesses. These connections may be due to the fact that the immune system is not functioning properly when you're tired, and the body can't heal as well, but it's also possible that a lack of sleep itself can be an indicator of a more serious underlying condition.

The bottom line is, if you are experiencing sleep loss on a regular basis, take steps to correct it, including having a checkup to look for more serious issues. Don't try to power through with coffee and energy drinks, and the "Sleep when you're dead" mantra. Your long-term health may be at stake, and "when you're dead" may happen sooner rather than later.

Don't neglect your mental health. This is crucial. Don't just think that you can "tough things out" and "deal with it" if you're having a rough time of things emotionally. Maybe you can, but be willing to consider that there be may underlying causes. No amount of free time is going to help you if you don't feel mentally in good shape, and you won't likely be able to make the changes suggested in this book unless you feel good enough to do so.

Anxiety, depression, and other mental health issues are very real and can take a considerable toll on you. They can completely prevent you from doing what you want to do and feeling in control of your time or anything else. Here is a brief overview of both depression and anxiety symptoms. Again, this is not meant to diagnose any specific problem, and if you are experiencing any of these symptoms, please take the time to see a qualified professional.

Symptoms of depression can include:

- **Depression is not just feeling sad.** It's a complex series of signs and symptoms that can have several causes, and can affect every aspect of one's life.

- **Feeling hopeless and helpless:** No matter what happens, the individual may still feel still that everything is all hopeless or pointless. Even good things are just a momentary respite before something bad happens again, as it surely will.

- **Anger:** A person with depression may have anger that is unfocused. They may feel irritable all the time, have a short temper, and be more likely to snap at others over minor things.

- **Lack of interest in daily activities:** Things that were once fun and enjoyable may lose their appeal. Hobbies, music, and even food and sex may start to seem mundane and uninteresting. Your partner or your friends may notice your lack of interest in things you once enjoyed.

- **Lack of self-worth:** Depression can leave one feeling that they have no value. They may feel guilty about things that aren't their fault or be filled with self-criticism, and maybe assume that everyone else feels the same way about them. They may try to look for ways to make this a self-fulfilling prophecy.

- **Insomnia:** Depression is yet another cause of insomnia, but sometimes depression can lead to its opposite: sleeping too much. A desire to stay in bed all day, a feeling of lethargy, and a lack of motivation are all classic signs of depression.

- **Reckless behaviors:** Those with depression sometimes engage in more dangerous or self-destructive behaviors. These can be anything from substance abuse to speeding in one's car to reckless gambling and extreme sports taken to the literal extreme.

- **Suicidal thoughts or actions:** Unfortunately, those with depression may think about ending their lives or attempt to do so, seeing it as their only option. If you experience any of these thoughts, please call for help now. Phone numbers and online resources are listed in the back of the book.

STOP SUICIDE

- **Attention issues:** Someone with depression may have difficulty making decisions, or concentrating on anything for more than a short period of time. It can also affect one's memory.

Anxiety is not just about being anxious. Like depression, it can be multilayered and can affect anyone. We've all experienced anxiety at some point, most often in response to a stressful event, such as an impending argument, speaking in front of others, etc. For most, it passes when the event subsides. But more serious forms of anxiety can persist. They outlast the events that caused them and intrude into one's daily life, often lasting for weeks or months. These can be diagnosed as a generalized anxiety disorder.

Symptoms of anxiety can include:

- **Worrying to excess:** We all worry about things. But when that worry becomes chronic, continual, and involves things over which we have little to no control, it can become a big problem. Usually the worry is all out of proportion to the problem. If the worry continues for over six months and affects the person most of the time, it's considered a sign of a general disorder.

- **Being self-conscious:** The individual's worry may include fearing how others see them. They may feel incompetent, inadequate, not as good as everyone else, all of which provokes even more worry and anxiousness.

- **Frequent agitation:** The body may be in a state of stress or heightened alert. The sympathetic nervous system is overstimulated, and the person may be shaky, sweat, have a dry mouth, a racing heart, and other symptoms of nervousness.

- **Feeling irritable:** Being anxious usually also means being irritable. It's not a pleasant feeling, and people who are experiencing anxiety may be more prone to anger and to snap at others.

- **Feeling panicked:** Panic attacks are one of the key symptoms of anxiety disorder. They can come about for seemingly no reason and produce the same symptoms as agitation, but with the addition of a fear, even terror, that something horrible is going to happen. Or there may be nothing that is the focus, only the feeling of fear. Frequent panic attacks are possibly a sign of a panic disorder.

- **A desire for isolation:** We all need to be alone sometimes, but anxiety can make that desire more intense, since it's usually motivated less by fatigue or a need to hibernate, often by worry or fear of being judged by others in social situations, or of embarrassing oneself in public, or any other negative possibility that one can imagine. As a result of these fears, the individual may just try to avoid social situations altogether, making up excuses and just not going, even if they want to.

- **Irrational fears and worries:** Everyone knows about phobias, and we sometimes use the word in a joking context, but for people with genuine phobias, it's no joke. Having an irrational fear and anxiety about something that prevents a person from doing what they want or succeeding is a severe hindrance to their quality of life. They vary in degree of severity. A fear of spiders or snakes probably won't impact someone too much (except maybe when camping or being outdoors), but a general fear of going outside would be devastating.

If you suspect that you are dealing with something beyond fatigue, a few bad days, a general worry, or a case of the blahs, you owe it to yourself and your loved ones to seek help. There's absolutely no shame in reaching out to a qualified professional for an assessment. Not every mental health issue requires medication or therapy, though again, there is nothing wrong with these if you need them. Taking back control of your mental health is one of the best things you can do for yourself, and one of the most generous gifts you can offer your loved ones. It will also let you gain control back over your time and use it the way you want to.

Please consider reaching out and getting help. You're not alone and you don't have to suffer. The "Online Resources" portion of the Resources section at the back of the book offers useful websites for further information. People are waiting to help you.

[

"Care's an enemy of life."

—WILLIAM SHAKESPEARE

]

[CHAPTER 4:]
PROCRASTINATION: THE GREAT ENEMY

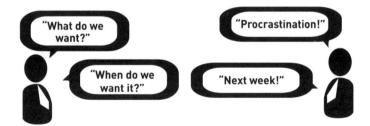

As noted earlier in the book, we always seem to find numerous ways of putting things off, or of convincing ourselves that tomorrow will be better, or next week we'll have more time to do something. The problem is, tomorrow never comes. There is always something new that comes up to distract us, keeps us from getting on with our plans and goals, or prevents us from getting our work done. So putting off things until later is almost always a bad idea. This can be anything from ignoring a work deadline because it's too overwhelming to failing to have an uncomfortable conversation with a friend because we fear the outcome. Fear of negative outcomes can often lead to putting things off even longer, only delaying the inevitable.

There's no doubt that procrastination is bad for the soul, but we do it anyway. We even joke about it and hold it up as if it's a virtue. This chapter will look at some of the reasons why we put things off, what some of the biggest culprits are, and steps you can take to minimize the procrastination threat and get back in control.

> ## "While we are postponing, life speeds by."
>
> **—SENECA**

WHY WE PROCRASTINATE; IT MAY NOT BE WHY YOU THINK

We all do it. Some do it more than others. Some have elevated it to an art form. But it rarely does anyone any good. Since procrastinating is such a universal bad habit, what are the driving forces behind it? Why do we leave things until later, even if we know it would be better to address them now? Here are some thoughts, based on psychological studies and assessments.

- **Procrastinating is not about being lazy.** This is a common misconception. The belief is that someone puts something off simply because they don't feel like doing it. Surprisingly, this is most often not the case. In fact, procrastinating can often be about doing something—anything—else rather than the task at hand. Someone needs to write an important report, but ends up rearranging the books on their bookshelves, for example, or spends the afternoon researching recipes instead of making an important phone call. We can be remarkably good at expending quite a lot of energy avoiding things we don't want to do!

- **Procrastination is not rational.** We know that by avoiding the task, it's only going to get worse. Yet we do it anyway. Why? Because procrastination is not a rational action. Dr. Fuschia Sirois, a psychology professor at the University of Sheffield, says, "It doesn't make sense to do something you know is going to have negative consequences." And yet, here we are.

- **Procrastination is often about not being able to deal with emotions wrapped up in a task.** Dr. Sirois continues: "People engage in this irrational cycle of chronic procrastination because of an inability to manage negative moods around a task." There can be any number of reasons why we might feel negative about the work in front of us. Maybe it's just distasteful: cleaning the sink or the toilet is hardly the most exciting thing you can do in your day off. But it might also be bound up in our own feelings of self-doubt and lack of worth. If we've been assigned an important work task, maybe we don't feel up to the challenge. Maybe we feel like we're an imposter, not good enough, and if we attempt this job, everyone will finally see what a fraud we are. It's a bit more complex than being lazy, isn't it?

- **Procrastination can come from a lack of motivation.** Tied up with our self-worth, we need to feel at least somewhat motivated to get things done. But our negative emotions, anxieties, and so forth about the task can interfere and leave us very unmotivated. Lack of motivation can also come from external factors, such as being overworked, not getting any credit, or not being  paid enough. All of these negative factors will feed into whatever doubts and fears we already have, creating a perfect mix of blah that will cause us to put off the task. Think about it: If you're going the extra mile for something, and no one is going to care, why should you bother? It's a great way to lose motivation quickly.

- **Procrastination can come from a lack of will to do something.** Willpower can be a key component of getting past procrastination. That doesn't mean a person is weak if they can't just power through it—quite the opposite. Someone who's been naturally good at things in their life (they did well in school, had a knack for some skill, etc.) may now be faced with a task that they can't do as easily. This is a surefire scenario for putting it off, since the brain is suddenly confronting confusing messages about the work needed to accomplish the task.

- **Procrastination can force us to face our fears.** Those negative emotions can be difficult for us to deal with. We may fear that if we try to finish a project, we'll just fail anyway, and then we'll be fired or everyone will think poorly of us. But here's an interesting thought: What if we finish a big project and it succeeds? We might be given a whole new set of responsibilities, people might expect more from us, and no one will realize that it might have just been a onetime fluke. We end up spending all our time focusing on the outcome (for good or bad), rather than the process of getting there. And with no focus on the process, the task just keeps getting put off.

- **Procrastination can come from other sources.** Putting things off can be caused by a number of factors, including: being a perfectionist (not willing to let it go), lack of a specified goal or outcome (why bother if we don't know what it's for?), a mental health issue such as depression, anxiety, or ADHD (which may need medical attention), or feeling disconnected from one's surroundings for any number of reasons.

THE EFFECTS OF ONGOING PROCRASTINATION

Putting off the occasional work project until the last minute probably won't affect you all that much at first. But if it becomes a habit, it can lead to all sorts of negative consequences, beyond putting your job in jeopardy or alienating your friends. Here are some effects of procrastination that you might find surprising.

- **It can harm your job and career.** You  may have skated through by doing your college research papers the night before they were due, and slipping by with mediocre grades and getting your degree, but how will that behavior translate into your professional life? Honestly, probably not very well, if you do everything at the last minute just because it has to get done. You're going to make mistakes, and people will notice. Maybe you'll be able to pull it off a few times, but eventually you'll slip up, you won't finish on time, or someone will see something wrong, and it's going to come back on you. Do this too many times, and you'll be out of a job.

- **You'll waste even more time.** You may think that delaying a project buys you time to do other tasks, and justify your procrastination with this; it might even be true at first. But ultimately if you're not giving your attention to the big projects that need it, all your work is going to suffer. In the bigger view, such as in your personal life, if you put off doing something that you should do now, how long will you let it go? A year? Two years?

Five years? What if you finally get around to doing something and feel regret that you could have started it years ago?

- **You will potentially miss good opportunities.** In both your professional and personal life, you run a huge risk of missing out on important things if you put them off. If you had the chance to take on new training but neglected to do it, a new job or promotion might come up requiring that skill that you didn't get around to learning. In your personal life, how many times have you put off saying something that needed to be said and then lost your chance? Maybe you needed to tell an elderly relative that you love them, but they passed away before you got around to it. Maybe you wanted to ask someone out on a date, but chickened out or came up with excuses not to, and now they're with someone else.

- **Your self-esteem will probably get worse.** If you are avoiding something because you fear it will all go wrong or because you fear it will all go right, just imagine what will happen if you keep doing it. If you know that you need to tackle a job or a problem, not doing it will only make you feel worse about yourself. You'll start blaming yourself for being inadequate, not capable, or any number of other deficiencies. If you're dealing with depression or another mental health issue, you probably already have some sense of how this feels.

- **It can affect how others see you.** In a professional sense, you may begin to get a reputation for being unreliable. If your coworkers can't trust you to get the job done, it's going to damage your working relationship and may put your job in danger if your boss isn't happy with what you're doing. In your personal life, putting things off too often can disappoint or hurt your friends and family, damage your personal relationships, and make you seem less trustworthy.

- **You may not make good decisions.** If you leave projects until the last minute and then have to work on them in a rush, you're less likely to be able to review them objectively, because you simply won't have time to consider every factor. You'll be making choices based on a deadline, rather than on informed information, and it's more likely that those choices will be poor or at least not as good as they could have been. This can also be true in your personal life, because you'll be making decisions based on stress and emotions, rather due to informed or rational reasons.

- **It can seriously affect your heath.** Recent studies have shown that regular procrastination can lead to serious levels of stress over time, which in turn can cause or aggravate cardiovascular issues and high blood pressure. Further, if you have a tendency to procrastinate about work or personal issues, research suggests you will be far more likely to put off going to the doctor, whether you have symptoms or not, and for the same reasons that you procrastinate in other areas of your life: fear of the results. You may also be less inclined to exercise or eat better ("I'll start next week"), contributing to overall poor health. Other studies have shown that chronic procrastinators are more susceptible to colds and the flu, as well as insomnia and indigestion problems—all no doubt stress-related. The takeaway is: procrastination is dangerous to your physical as well as your mental well-being!

- **It will make you unhappy.** In addition to everything else, chronic procrastinators frequently report that they are less satisfied and happy than others. The Procrastination Research Group at Carleton University (Ottawa) conducted a survey about procrastination and its effects. In answer to the question "To what extent is procrastination having a negative impact on your happiness?" 46 percent of respondents answered that procrastinating has a significant impact on feelings of being happy. Eighteen percent of those responded that the effect was "extreme." In short, putting things off will likely not make you feel better and has a good chance of making you feel much worse.

TEN WAYS TO WATCH OUT FOR BOREDOM!

We're all at risk of getting bored, especially if the job is repetitive, or not challenging or stimulating enough. A recent study showed that employees can feel bored at work for more than ten hours out of the week, a full quarter of their work time. The problem with boredom is that we lose valuable time, either by watching the clock and waiting for the day to end, or looking for ways to stop the bored feelings while not addressing the work or the tasks we need to do. If you're feeling a bit stagnant at work, what can you do to move beyond it and make sure you're not wasting time just being bored? Here are some suggestions.

1. **Try to think about your task in a new way.**
   What might your project be like to someone who's never seen it before? How would you explain it to them? Is there something about it that's unusual or odd that would seem strange to an outsider? Think about how your work might be beneficial to others, especially if you're creating something that will be consumed in some way by the public or other businesses. Try bringing that kind of outside thinking to your task and see if it gives you a novel way of approaching it.

2. **Take a quick break.** If you're slogging through something and it's getting nowhere, it probably won't do you any good to keep at it. If you can take a quick two-minute break, it might be enough to get you past the stuck phase. Stand up, go get some water, or visit a coworker and ask

them a question you've been meaning to. Anything to break the routine and get your mind to a different place for a few minutes can help.

3. **Get out of your surroundings.** Being able to do this will depend on the kind of work you do, and the nature of your office or other environment. But if you have the option to move around a bit, try getting away from your desk and taking your work to a new area. Even if it's in the same workspace, a literal change of scene might be enough to get you out of your funk and get moving again. If you have flexible work time or work from home, get out and go for a short walk. Any kind of break and change will do you good.

4. **Think about making it more challenging.** Sometimes, boredom is caused by a task being too easy or routine. Look for ways to diversify it and try to think about how you can challenge yourself. Is there something you can do that will make the task more efficient or produce a better result? Try seeing if there are any problems about it to solve. Even something simple like writing a report: Is there a better way to approach it? Can you make it more interesting or more useful? Look for problems to solve, and your boredom may evaporate.

5. **Be aware of your need for novelty.** Extroverts and those known as sensation seekers frequently need the new in order to feel stimulated. They are more prone to boredom, simply because something is familiar and no longer exciting. Unfortunately, not all work is going to be exciting. But if you are aware of your personality type, you can work on ways to mitigate that boredom. On the other hand, people with ADHD can find it difficult to concentrate for long periods of time and can get bored or frustrated easily.

6. **Clean up.** It may seem simple, but sometimes a good declutter of your workspace can do wonders to get you back in the game and renew your

enthusiasm. If you're overflowing with papers, files, and junk, try getting your space a bit more organized. A cleaner and more efficient workspace can be inspiring. This same rule also applies to virtual cleaning, like your email inbox or your computer desktop. The clearer your space, the better you will feel.

7. Have fun. Maybe you can test yourself to see how many reports you can get done in thirty minutes. Reward yourself with a coffee or a donut if you meet your goal. Maybe you can pretend you're working on some top-secret project or racing to save the world. Try creating some sort of fun competition with a coworker. It sounds silly, but these kinds of role-playing games can offer a way to approach your work with a new attitude. Even better, no one else has to know!

8. Take care of your health. Feeling sluggish or unmotivated at work can have its roots in not getting enough sleep, poor eating habits, and any number of other seemingly unrelated behaviors in our personal lives. Take the time to look after yourself during your personal time, and you'll probably feel more motivated during your work time.

9. Talk with others and remind yourself of what you do. You may be bored because you feel like your work has no purpose. It's good to check in with your coworkers and see how they are doing as well. You may find that more than one person has the same feeling. Brainstorm what you can do to fix the problem. By comparing notes and sharing stories, you not only won't feel alone, but also it may remind you that what you're doing is not useless and has a bigger purpose after all.

10. **Be aware of your current situation.** If you feel trapped in your job, you're more likely to be bored. Ask yourself how you feel and what your current state of mind is regarding your work. If you feel like you have no room for advancement, or your skills are not being utilized or appreciated, you're far more likely to feel bored with the tasks that you do have. You may need to sit with this for a while and assess your career and where you are, and more importantly, where you want to be. Your boredom might be a clear sign that you're ready to move on, and you should start thinking about looking for another job, one that will challenge you better.

> **"It's how we spend our time here and now, that really matters. If you are fed up with the way you have come to interact with time, change it."**
>
> **—MARCIA WIEDER**

HOW TO BEAT THE PROCRASTINATION PROBLEM: TEN STRATEGIES

You may think that it's hopeless, and you're doomed to procrastinate until your final day, which, with any luck, you'll also be able to put off. But in reality, there are several actions you can take right now to ditch the procrastination stagnation and get things moving again (assuming you don't put those off, too!). These suggestions work for both business and personal issues.

1. **Make things more urgent.** We tend to only pay attention to what is right in front of us, so if we're faced with a task that's not due for ten days or two weeks, we will be more likely to ignore it until it becomes urgent, like the night before it's due! This is probably due to evolutionary reasons; it made much more sense for survival to be focused on what was immediate. The solution is to see the task in terms of a bigger picture, one that affects you. How would starting this project right now help you today? What advantage is there to getting that report in ahead of the deadline? It might simply be that you'll be less stressed or have more free time. Make the outcome a bit more immediate to your needs, and you'll start to see its importance.

2. **Start small.** Don't try to do it all at once. If you've spent your life putting things off, you're not suddenly going to change this behavior overnight. Trying to take on a huge task right away will just leave you feeling overwhelmed, and you'll likely give up and be even more frustrated. Pick something that you know you need to do but that won't take long to actually finish up, and do that first. Then pick another small thing and accomplish that task. If the project is confusing or you need more information to start, make that your first step. The idea is to get used to being on time little by little, so that it becomes a new habit.

3. **Break things down.** When you are facing a large project or task, don't try to see the whole thing all at once. Break it down into smaller, more doable parts. Say you're writing a 1,500-word report (or research paper, whatever), due in ten days. Start right away: divide the task up into sections: research and background reading (do for, say, thirty minutes at a time), outline the paper, commit to writing 150 words at a time (a few times a day), review, edit, and submit. Do you need to clean the kitchen? Start with the cupboards only, or just clean the stove. The next day, do something else. Give it fifteen minutes of your time daily, and in a week, it might be done. Starting and staying small can be a very effective way of not getting overwhelmed.

4. **Remove distractions.** Turn off your phone. Completely off. Unless you need it for some specific work reason or a potential emergency, it's just going to drag you away from the task at hand. This also goes for internet and social media (see below, page 120). They are massive time-wasters that will drag you back in again and again. If you have a noisy work environment, try using headphones or earbuds, but make sure that any music you're listening to is also not overly distracting.

5. **Create realistic timelines.** If a project needs to be finished in ten days, allow ten days for it, with descriptions of what needs to be done each day. This follows from breaking things down into manageable portions. In this case, you'll be able to see what each portion is and when it needs to be done. Focus only on that portion that day, unless you get ahead and want to do a bit more. Otherwise, it's fine to leave tomorrow's tasks for tomorrow.

6. **Create realistic deadlines.** If you don't have a deadline (say, you're cleaning your kitchen), set one for yourself. How long will it actually take to do it all? If you want that kitchen clean, make a commitment to working on it for twenty minutes every night until Saturday, for example. It gives you a defined goal to work toward, while not seeming unrealistic.

7. **Do the difficult things first.** As we've seen, it's often best if you tackle the more difficult parts of the task first and get them out of the way. The project will then get easier as you go along. Since things sometimes have a tendency to get into a slump in the middle, if you're still facing a big upward-hill climb halfway through, you might get discouraged and not finish. However, remember that sometimes if you are faced with starting something difficult, you might not even begin at all, so if you know this is true about yourself, take some of the easier parts of the task and work on those first, to give yourself a little momentum. Just be sure to save some easier work for later on!

8. **Have a partner to keep you on track.** One of the best ways of keeping yourself motivated is to partner up with someone. This person can be a master of their time, or they might even be a fellow procrastinator. What's important is that you each have your own goals to meet and tasks to finish. It's a great way to check in on each other and keep each other on the path. You'll develop a greater sense of responsibility knowing that you have to check in with your buddy. It can

motivate you to help the other person out, too, if they get stuck or start falling back into putting things off.

9. **Tell the world.** Well, maybe not the whole world, but let your friends and/or coworkers know what you're doing. As with having a partner, by telling others about your goals (even the goal of ending your procrastinating ways), you make yourself accountable. People will invariably ask you how you're doing, how the project is going, if you're actually going to the gym three days a week, and so on, especially if you ask them to check in with you. Unless you're prepared to flat-out lie to them, you'll have to be honest and keep them updated.

10. **Reward yourself for a job well done.** A simple little trick, but offering yourself a reward for a job well done on time or getting around to starting something you've been meaning to can be a carrot dangling in front of you that makes you want to move forward. Tell yourself that if you finish that report on time, you'll have a nice coffee or tea. If you finally clean the kitchen, you'll binge a few episodes of a show on a streaming service. It doesn't have to be something grand; a little reward can be enough. But tying it to a project or chore you need to do is a nice way to motivate yourself to get it done.

FIVE WAYS TO MEET DEADLINES WITHOUT THE STRESS

Procrastination almost always leads to having to do things at the last minute. Some people thrive on this and do their best work under the heat of a looming deadline. If you're one of those people, then this section probably doesn't concern you. But most of us probably procrastinate knowing that leaving things until later will only make things worse. Yet, we still do it. If you want to avoid the extreme stress of an all-night marathon to get something done by its due date, here are some suggestions to make your finish a little less of a white-knuckle experience.

1. **Try to estimate timings for all tasks.** This will take some practice, but if you can work out about how much time you'll need for each component of the project, you'll have a better sense of how long the whole thing will take. Certain tasks will undoubtedly take longer than others, so you'll need to devote more time to them. Again, the more you do this, the more intuitive you'll become. It will give you a better sense of what needs to be done if you're facing a big deadline.

2. **Be realistic about what you can do.** Take stock of yourself, your skills, and your energy levels. What can you realistically accomplish in a given day or work period? Overestimating your own abilities will only make things harder later on, if you start falling behind. If you know you

can only devote two hours to a single task before your brain gives out and you need to switch to something else, don't program in four hours of work on that topic. This is where the practice of chunking can come in handy (see page 23).

3. **Be realistic about the deadline.** How realistic is the deadline, given what you know about yourself and your available time? If you have imposed the deadline on yourself, you may need to adjust it and move it back. If the deadline is one that has been imposed on you, say, at work, you might need to see if it's possible to negotiate 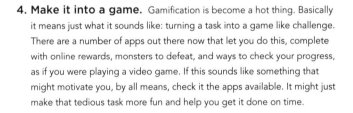 an extension. Your workplace might be amenable to moving the due date back, if you can show how a few extra days or a week will be beneficial. If it's a college deadline, you'll probably have no choice but to step up and meet it as best you can, using the techniques given in this chapter.

4. **Make it into a game.** Gamification is become a hot thing. Basically it means just what it sounds like: turning a task into a game like challenge. There are a number of apps out there now that let you do this, complete with online rewards, monsters to defeat, and ways to check your progress, as if you were playing a video game. If this sounds like something that might motivate you, by all means, check it the apps available. It might just make that tedious task more fun and help you get it done on time.

5. **Ask for help.** There's no shame in asking for help. If you're facing a deadline you know you can't meet, talk to your boss about ways that someone could assist you. If the deadline can't be moved, this is the next best solution. Just make sure that you are clear about the kind of help you need, and who could best be of assistance.

THE ONLINE TIME-WASTING SCOURGE AND HOW TO RECOGNIZE IT

Unfortunately, our lives are ruled by the internet and online activities. For better and worse, we are each continually plugged into our own personal Matrix, with faces glued to cell phones and other devices. The joke about it being a different kind of zombie apocalypse is not too far off. And all of this logging in, checking statuses, reading updates, getting texts, and a zillion other things we do adds up, mostly, to a phenomenal waste of time. Sure, we can use connections for good purposes, but if you really ask yourself how much time you *need* to be spending online, you'll find that you could be doing better things with your life. Here are some of the time-wasters you should look out for, and ways to minimize them.

- **Random internet surfing:** This is the classic action we now take when we're bored. We need something to entertain us, so we start clicking randomly, go down rabbit holes, watch three videos on alpaca ranches in South America, and the next thing we know, two hours have gone by. Two precious hours that we could have been doing something better. Why do we do this? It has to do with brain

stimulation. Studies have shown that reward centers in the brain light up not only when experiencing a pleasurable act (such as eating or sex) but also when viewing pictures or other information, whether related to those acts or not. So, the internet is one endless source of mind stimulation! We can spend literally hours cruising around online, getting dopamine hit after dopamine hit, and before we know it, half the day is gone. Then we may hate ourselves for getting so sucked in, only to do it again a day or two later.

- **Social media:** Probably the biggest scourge of them all, social media was meant to connect people, to allow us to share things in our lives, and to meet new people all over the world. And yes, it can do those things, but how often do you hear people complain (or even complain yourself) about how social media sites are now just exercises in ego-stroking. We hear all this talk about influencers online, often with no clue as to who these people are, nor do we care. The thing is, social media isn't just annoying; it's actually having negative consequences for people. Various studies have shown that social media sites can affect people in bad ways.

- **Self-esteem:** Social media can cause huge hits to our sense of self-worth. We see everyone posting about the amazing things they're doing, the incredible lives they're leading, the awesome vacation they're on, and we despair about how mundane our own meager little existence is by comparison. But the big secret (that's not so secret) is that everyone is posting their best images and experiences. What they're showing you isn't their whole life, just a heavily edited version that they want others to see. We can all pick out just the great things and post about them, but that doesn't make them the total of our lives. Within our closer friend circle, we may all feel more comfortable about posting the bad aspects of our lives or even asking for help, so that's something of a counterbalance.

- **Life experience:** The need to present oneself at one's best can be affected by the presence of social media requirements. If you are traveling somewhere, are you really taking everything in, or are you just looking for the best picture to post to your profile? Did you watch the street performance, or just record it on your phone so you can upload it later? Think about how social media may be making you miss out on real experiences.

- **Attention span:** Social media addiction can lead to endless flicking through one's feed in search of the next thing. Like the dopamine hit mentioned above, it can lead to difficulty in concentrating on anything for more than a few seconds, because there is always some new post to check out or some new headline that needs to be read. How often on social media sites do you see someone comment on a news headline when they clearly haven't read the story? They only had the attention span to read the headline. And that's the problem.

- **Isolation:** Social media is meant to bring people together, to make new connections and foster new dialogues. But for a lot of people, it only makes them feel more lonely and isolated. Perhaps they get more in the habit of interacting with people online than actually going out and socializing in the real world. Another problem is fear of missing out (FOMO). If we're always hearing about the allegedly amazing things that others are doing, we can start to see our lives as empty and boring by comparison. They probably aren't, but we're getting a skewed sense of things and maybe feeling like we're not living an interesting life at all, unlike everyone else.

- **Physical health issues:** Social media addicts have reported any number of ailments, from insomnia and sleep loss (staying up too late), to neck problems from looking down at their phones so much! Headaches, eye strain, and even sore thumbs and arms are all consequences of being glued to a phone or other device all day, to say nothing of skipping exercise, getting fresh air, eating properly, and other potential hazards.

- **Mental health issues:** Surveys have shown that as many as one-third of social media users feel depressed or anxious, and many of these respondents have thought that leaving social media behind, at least for a while, would help them. This turns out to be true. Studies suggest that taking periodic cold-turkey breaks from social media can do our mental health some real good. Too much social media can also lead to self-absorbed feelings, if all one wants to do is post endless selfies to get that dopamine hit of likes and praise. A far bigger concern is cyberbullying, which is rampant on social media sites, and its terrible effects on one's mental health and well-being.

- **Personal email:** At work, your use of personal email will probably be limited, and you likely won't be allowed to use your work email for personal reasons. So, you'll probably be less distracted by incoming personal emails. But email in your home life can also take up a lot of time. If you're getting bombarded by emails, it might be time to start sorting through them and seeing how many are necessary.

- **Texting:** Texting has become the one of the main ways that people communicate. It's quickly outpacing talking on the phone and shows no signs of slowing down. Yet maybe it should? If texting is taking up a lot of your time, you may need to put the phone down, turn it off, and leave it for a while. The problem, of course, is that even if you're committed to taking breaks from your phone, your friend and colleagues may not be so determined. It's one thing to turn your phone off for two hours and work, exercise, or whatever you want to do, but if you turn it back on and get swamped with seventy-seven texts, you're going to have to spend time sifting through them, whether you want to or not.

LEARNING TO DISCONNECT FROM THE ONLINE WORLD

So, with all of these online distractions taking away our precious time, what can we do to minimize them and still make good use of online time when we want or need it? There are a number of ways for each type of online distraction.

- **Internet:** Internet surfing is a classic, mindless way to waste time that could be better spent doing other things. Sometimes, it's fun to just sit and cruise for a while, but it can quickly become a bad habit. If you'd like to spend less time doing mindless things online, here are some helpful tips.

  - **Turn it off.** It seems simple, but just limiting your access to the internet can make it easier not to go on it. If you really need to get a project done, a paper written, or whatever you need to do, try just disconnecting and leaving it alone for a while. It'll still be there when you get back, we promise.

  - **Block sites you regularly visit.** If you know there are sites that you waste a lot of time on (social media and others), you can install apps and programs that will block you from accessing them at specified times so that you can get your work done. It's kind of like parental controls for adults, except you're being your own parent. At work, you may have a computer that is designated for work only; this is good, since it will prevent you from being tempted to slip off into internet-land whenever boredom creeps in.

- **Save sites for later viewing.** It's easy to go down a rabbit hole and read one article after another, even if you only intended to read one. Sites are set up to tempt you to stay on them. Download and use an app that will let you save articles and pages for later browsing. The point is to limit the amount of time you spend online at any given moment, so that you can use your time better, whether for work or leisure. And you may find that when you return to those saved pages, you're not as interested in reading them as you thought you were.

- **Assess what's really necessary.** As mentioned above, cruising for new sites and stimulation gives us a brief dopamine hit, but then we want more, so we stay online and keep looking up new things. Try to make your internet use more meaningful. Before just clicking random links because of some flashy headline, stop and 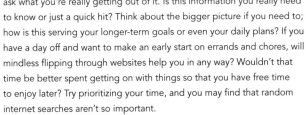 ask what you're really getting out of it. Is this information you really need to know or just a quick hit? Think about the bigger picture if you need to; how is this serving your longer-term goals or even your daily plans? If you have a day off and want to make an early start on errands and chores, will mindless flipping through websites help you in any way? Wouldn't that time be better spent getting on with things so that you have free time to enjoy later? Try prioritizing your time, and you may find that random internet searches aren't so important.

- **Try slowing things down.** That dopamine hit often comes because we are rapidly scanning through many pages and sites, in a desperate attempt for more entertainment. But consider committing to just a few pages or articles and spending time with them; read the whole story, not just the headline. You'll get much more out of them, and you may find that your craving is satisfied. If so, you'll spend less time online in general and make the time you do use it more meaningful and useful.

- **Social media:** Social media is probably your biggest waste of time. Just because everyone is using one or more platforms doesn't mean that you need to be on them or checking up on them all the time. It's fine to dip in and see what's happening, but you need to make a genuine effort to distance yourself from these sites and claim back your valuable time. Here are some suggestions for how to do it.

  - **Total up the amount of time you spend on social media.** Make an effort to calculate just how much time you spend on social media sites every day. You'll probably be shocked. After you learn the awful truth, make a commitment to cut that time in half. Yes, in half.

  - **Total up the number of social media sites you're on.** How many is it? Two? Four? More? Ask yourself just how useful these are. Which one(s) do you genuinely use the most? Which ones do you have an account on that you barely look at or don't like using, even if you feel obligated to? Reduce those or eliminate them entirely. Stick only with the sites that you genuinely need or enjoy using.

  - **Look at how many people you follow and consider reducing the number.** Do you need to follow or be "friends" with that many people? Is it OK to unfollow them or at least mute them? The point here is to clear your feed of clutter and posts from people you don't know and don't want to read anything from anyway. The fewer new posts that are in your feed, the less time you'll spend scrolling.

  - **Post things that are meaningful.** Before cluttering up the virtual space with a shared post or a nonsense post that doesn't matter, ask yourself if this post really needs to go out. The occasional funny posting is fine, but if you're cluttering up your friend's timelines with endless shares, maybe you're not only wasting your time, but theirs as well.

  - **Eliminate social media notifications.** This holds true for texting as well (see below). Whether you're browsing via a phone or a laptop or other device, get rid of social media notifications, whether by text or email. It's highly unlikely that there's anything you desperately need to know.

- **Delete social media apps from your phone.** This may seem like a more drastic measure, but if you are having real issues staying off social media sites during the day, remove access to them from your phone. That way, you'll only be able to access them after work via your laptop, desktop, or other device. The content will still be there (honest!), and you will probably find that you don't need to keep up with every post and update; just dipping in for a while will be fine.

• **Email:** Email is less and less a way that people keep in touch for socializing, but you may still find that you have endless numbers of emails to get through every day, on top of whatever your work requires you to sift through. Even at work, you may feel yourself being  inundated with emails and struggling with a process that could probably be more efficient and streamlined. If you'd like to spend less time emailing, here are some ideas.

- **Be careful about how you use email to begin with.** In a work situation (or even a personal one), watch out that you don't turn emails into back-and-forth conversations. If you're scheduling a meeting, for example, don't ask everyone what their best times are. You'll get a pile of answers that will conflict and even more clutter in your inbox. Use an online scheduling tool or calendar and direct people to respond there. Try not to make emails open conversations at all. Instead of ending the email with a question (inviting a response), end with a statement: "I'll call you on Wednesday morning so that we can discuss things more."

- **"Train" people to email you less and less.** One way to do this is by not responding right away. It's OK to wait on a response unless it's absolutely urgent, comes from your boss, is an emergency, etc. But if someone at work emails you asking a question, try not getting back to them for a few hours. You might just find that in the intervening time, they figured it out for themselves, and that's one less email you have to write or problem you need to solve. Over time, those people might email you less.

- **Limit the number of times you check email every day.** Unless it's a matter of urgency or your job requires it, try to keep the times for checking email to a minimum, maybe twice a day or three times at most. It's unlikely that there's anything that urgent that needs your immediate attention, and this can go a long way to helping "train" others, as set out above.

- **Use an autoresponder, even when you're there.** These don't have to be just for vacations. You can set up one when you're busy with other tasks and let the sender know that you'll reply to them when you can. It's a courteous way of saying "don't bother me right now" and will prevent repeat emails if they don't hear back in the next half hour.

- **Limit the length of the emails you send.** Try to keep them fairly short and to the point, rather than getting into long-winded monologues, which may invite long-winded responses. Say what you need to say and don't invite long conversations.

- **Never hit "reply all" to a group conversation unless it's genuinely needed.** This has been an email gripe since the 1990s. How often have you received an email that quotes the entire original post and has some useless comment at the bottom like "I agree"? And when you get ten of these in your inbox, you're ready to smash something. The fact that this still occurs is maddening enough, so don't do it yourself. If you see others doing it, gently remind them not to.

- **Unsubscribe to newsletters.** You've probably signed up for several of them. Take stock of how many you receive weekly and ask yourself just how necessary they are? This goes for both your personal and professional email accounts. There might be a few that are worth keeping, but if some of them are sending you mails every day that you don't even bother to read, just get rid of them. There are programs that will let you mass-unsubscribe if you are signed up on a lot of lists. Whittle the list down to something more manageable, and only keep the newsletters you really want and actually bother to read.

- **Create templates for similar emails.** If you have to send the same kind of email over and over, many email programs will let you create a template email that you can customize as you need. That way, you won't have to retype the whole thing every time.

- **Organize your inbox.** Don't just let every email pile up in one folder. Create subfolders or alternate inboxes, grouped by subject, and be diligent about putting new emails into them; it will make them easier to find. Delete or archive old emails and keep your inbox clear! Just seeing a decluttered inbox will make you feel better and will save you time and effort later on.

- **Texting:** If you want to break the texting habit, you'll be in for something of an uphill battle, since almost everyone does it and expects everyone else to do it these days. As far as work-related texts go, you might be stuck with them, but for personal texts, you do have more control. Here are some ideas to wean yourself off being glued to your phone.

  - **Turn off notifications.** Yes, this means you'll be bombarded later on, but it will get you in the habit of not checking your phone every two minutes. The point is to take quality time away from it.

  - **Silence incoming texts.** There are apps that will notify the texter that you're unavailable for a period of time. This can be useful for them, too, so that they don't keep messaging you. The idea is to bring down the total number of texts to a more manageable level so that you don't have to spend ages on the phone.

- **Look at other apps to help cut down.** There are apps that will count the number of texts you send and receive, and even let you know when you're overdoing it. Having an objective "score" of the total number may surprise you.

- **Talk with your partner.** If you have a partner or spouse and you'd like to cut down on texting, please talk to them about it. Share your concerns and see if there is a way you can work out how to do it that's acceptable to both of you. It may even lead to spending more actual time together, which is a good thing!

- **Unlink to social media.** Do you really need a notification every time someone tweets a thing or posts to Instagram? No, you really don't. This is another good way to start decluttering the number of texts and notifications you receive.

- **Put your phone away while outside.** Every year, an alarming number of accidents strike people who are not paying attention while outside, because they have their noses in their phone, even while crossing streets. And that number is only going to increase. Leave your phone in your pocket or bag when walking from one place to another. Nothing is so important in a text that you need to risk your life for it! And if it is that important, stop somewhere and take care of it.

- **Never try to text while driving.** Never. It may not just be your time that you lose. There are even apps that will disable your phone while you're driving. If drive-texting is something you engage in from time to time, please do this. Your friends and loved ones will thank you for it.

- **Never text while drunk or otherwise impaired.** This is a recipe for disaster, since you may type something you'll regret later on. If you plan on drinking or indulging in anything that will cloud your judgment, turn your phone off and put it away.

- **Never text while you're angry or emotional.** Again you may type something you'll regret later. Take the time to cool down, think it over, whatever you have to do. Never let the urge to text interfere with the time you need to process something.

- **Ignore texts while you are doing something else.** If you are in the middle of a project, a run, a cleaning, a good book, leave the phone alone and ignore it. Finish what you're doing first; make yourself and your activities the priority. The text will still be there, but your time may not.

- **Take a "text break."** Make the decision to **not** text for twenty-four hours, or twelve hours, or whatever you think you can manage. Start with shorter time periods and work up to longer ones, if you need to. See if you can go a whole day. The point is that you might have an addiction, or at least a compulsion, so cutting it down will do you good.

- **Text less, and phone or meet up more.** Try to get together with people more often, if you can, rather than just texting them. Even if you can only talk on the phone with a friend for a few minutes, do it. The interactions will be much more meaningful and memorable.

- **Leave your phone off when you're out.** If you're, say, having dinner with friends, turn the phone off. Your attention should be on them, anyway, and it's rude to interrupt to check on something, unless you are expecting an important message, have a personal concern, etc. We see this happen all the time at restaurants and cafes, but ask yourself if it's really good manners? No, it really isn't. Disconnect and give your time to the people right in front of you.

RESOURCES

A short book like this can only give you so much information,
but there is a wealth of time management material out there,
both in print (and e-book form) and online. These selections
should be helpful in giving you expanded information. The online
suggestions offer links mental health resources.

FURTHER READING

There are many different approaches to time management, as we've seen in this book. The following works go into more detail, and will allow you to explore different ways to manage your time more efficiently, from getting more done during the day to defeating procrastination once and for all.

David Allen, *Getting Things Done: The Art of Stress-Free Productivity* (Penguin, 2015).

Jack Barrett, *Strategies and Tips for Time Management: Secrets to Organizing Yourself and Ending Procrastination* (Independently published, 2019).

Lee Cockerell, *Time Management Magic: How to Get More Done Every Day and Move from Surviving to Thriving* (Morgan James Publishing, 2019).

Debra Conn, *Time Management Strategy: The Proven 6 Step System to Easily Manage Multiple Projects, Take Control of Stress, and Make Time for Yourself* (Independently published, 2020).

Nate Daniels, *Managing Your Day Today: Increase Productivity, Build an Effective Routine and Become Mentally Strong: Habits, Motivation, Focus, Time Management, Organization, Procrastination* (Independently published, 2019).

Holly Reisem Hanna, *Time Management in 20 Minutes a Day: Simple Strategies to Increase Productivity, Enhance Creativity, and Make Your Time Your Own* (Althea Press, 2019).

Kevin Kruse, *15 Secrets Successful People Know about Time Management* (Kruse Group, 2015).

Jason Selk, Tom Bartow, and Matthew Rudy, *Organize Tomorrow Today: 8 Ways to Retrain Your Mind to Optimize Performance at Work and in Life* (Da Capo Lifelong Books, 2016).

Tiffany Shelton, *Five-Minute Focus: Exercises to Reduce Distraction, Improve Concentration, and Increase Performance* (Rockridge Pres, 2019).

Brian Tracy, *Eat That Frog!: 21 Great Ways to Stop Procrastinating and Get More Done in Less Time*, 3rd edition (Berrett-Koehler, 2017).

Bill Wilson, *7 Maxims of Time Management: Seven Timeless Truths That Will Enable You to Gain Control of Your Time and Your Life* (Independently published, 2020).

Damon Zahariades, *The Procrastination Cure: 21 Proven Tactics For Conquering Your Inner Procrastinator, Mastering Your Time, and Boosting Your Productivity!* (Independently published, 2017).

Damon Zahariades, *The Time Chunking Method: A 10-Step Action Plan For Increasing Your Productivity* (Independently published, 2017).

ONLINE RESOURCES FOR MENTAL HEALTH ISSUES

These resources are for mental health issues. They can be not only helpful but also lifesaving for people who need them. Please don't hesitate to reach out and get help if you need it.

10 mental health resources you never knew you had

An excellent listing of online resources for a variety of mental health concerns. Form the website: "Each province in Canada has its own comprehensive site where you can do online assessments to get more information about how you're feeling. You can also find easy to access information and quick facts on PTSD, depression, anxiety and many other disorders on each site, plus a directory for mental health services across your province."
theloop.ca/10-mental-health-resources-never-knew

Canadian Government: Mental health support

A government site providing links and phone numbers for mental health help, including for children and First Nations and Inuit.
canada.ca/en/public-health/services/mental-health-services/mental-health-get-help.html

Crisis Services Canada

A hotline for suicide prevention and support: 1.833.456.4566
Test "Start" to 45645, 4:00 p.m. to midnight, ET
crisisservicescanada.ca/en/

Mind Your Mind

An online resource for mental health issues. From the website: "mindyourmind exists in the space where mental health, wellness, engagement and technology meet. We work with community partners and young people aged 14 to 29 to co-create interactive tools and innovative resources to build capacity and resilience."
mindyourmind.ca

Mind Your Mind: Where to call

An online listing of important, lifesaving phone numbers.
mindyourmind.ca/help/where-call

ABOUT THE AUTHOR

Tim Rayborn is a writer, educator, historian, musician, and researcher, with more than twenty years of professional experience. He is a prolific author, with a number of books and articles to his name, and more on the way. He has written on topics from the academic to the amusing to the appalling, including medieval and modern history, the arts (music, theater, and dance), food and wine, business, social studies, and works for business and government publications. He's also been a ghostwriter for various clients.

Based in the San Francisco Bay Area, Tim lived in England for seven years, studying for an M.A. and Ph.D. at the University of Leeds. He has a strong academic background but enjoys writing for general audiences.

He is also an acclaimed classical and world musician, having appeared on more than forty recordings, and he has toured and performed in the United States, Canada, Europe, North Africa, and Australia over the last twenty-five years. During that time, he has learned much about the business of arts and entertainment, and how to survive and thrive when traveling and working in intense environments.

For more, visit timrayborn.com.

INDEX

A

acne, as sign of stress, 93

agenda for meetings, 61

alarms, 30, 31, 32

alone time, 70, 83

anger, as sign of depression, 98

anxiety, 97, 99, 100, 106, 135

apps for managing time, 27

attention issues, as sign of depression, 99

automating bill payments, 79

autoresponders, for managing email, 128

B

bedtime, 84

boredom, 59, 110–13, 124

breakfast, 19, 20, 30, 32, 33, 65

breaks, 22, 59, 65, 68, 83, 89, 90, 91, 110, 111

bulk, buying in, 79

busy times at stores, avoiding, 78

C

calendar, 26, 27, 37, 76, 127

chest pain, as sign of stress, 93

chores, 71, 76, 78, 86, 87, 117, 125

chunking time, 23, 24, 25, 38, 42, 78, 119, 134

commute, 33, 34, 35, 36, 63, 65, 81

D

deadlines, 21, 23, 24, 29, 37, 41, 47, 51, 53, 65, 68, 83, 95, 103, 109, 114, 116, 118–19

decluttering, 73, 111, 129, 130

delegating, 47, 55, 56

depressed immune system, from lack of sleep, 96

depression, 96–99, 106, 108, 123, 135

desire for isolation, as sign of anxiety, 100

digestive issues, as sign of stress, 94

distractions while working, 6, 23, 63, 71, 115, 124, 134

downtime, 39, 84, 87

driving, for commute, 35, 36

E

Eisenhower Decision Matrix, 41, 43

electronic stimulation, 83

emails, responding to, 43, 44, 45

errands, 24, 25, 71, 76, 78–80, 86, 87, 125

extrovert, 63, 70, 111

F

feeling hopeless and helpless, as sign of depression, 98

feeling irritable, as sign of anxiety, 100

feeling panicked, as sign of anxiety, 100

file-sharing programs, 26

flagging emails, 44

flexibility, 20, 65

fear of missing out (FOMO), 122

frequent agitation, as sign of anxiety, 100

frequent illness, as sign of stress, 93–94

G

gamifying, 59, 119

get-togethers, 75

gratitude journal, 84

H

headaches, as sign of stress, 92

hobbies, 84, 98

home life, 24, 73, 123

I

increased blood pressure, as sign of stress, 94

increased heart rate, as sign of stress, 94

insomnia, as sign of depression, 98

introvert, 63, 70

irrational fears and worries, as sign of anxiety, 100

Ivy Lee Method, 42

L

lack of alertness, from lack of sleep, 96

lack of interest in daily activities, as sign of depression, 98

lack of self-worth, as sign of depression, 98

listening to music, while working, 16

lowered libido, as sign of stress, 94

M

master list of tasks, 39

measurable goals, 50

meditation, 27, 28, 84, 87

meetings, 26, 29, 36, 38, 48, 60–62, 85, 127

memory loss, from lack of sleep, 96

mental health, 7, 95, 97, 101, 106, 108, 123, 132, 135

micro-breaks, 59

mindfulness, 84

mini-goals, 50

mini-meetings, 61

mini-vacation, 83, 86

minutes, from meetings, 62

multitasking, 14–16, 23, 46, 76

muscle tension, as sign of stress, 92

N

nonwork emails, 45

O

overcommitting, 50, 86

overloaded, 55, 67

overstimulation, 82

overtime, 65, 66, 67, 68

P

pain, as sign of stress, 93

password encryption program, 27

personal time, 20, 69, 83, 112

prioritizing, 6, 18, 21, 38, 40, 41, 43, 77, 86, 125

procrastination, 102–3, 104–6, 107–9, 114, 118, 133–34

productivity, 15, 34, 38, 42, 58–59, 87, 133, 134

project, workplace definition of, 53

public transit, for commute, 35

R

realistic goals, 49–51

reckless behaviors, as sign of depression, 98

risk for illness, from lack of sleep, 97

routine, 19–20, 21, 32, 37, 58, 81, 82, 133

S

schedules, 6, 17, 19, 20, 24, 31, 32, 37–39, 46–47, 49, 50, 52, 58, 64, 75, 85, 88, 95

self-consciousness, as sign of anxiety, 99

self-motivation, 64

skimming emails, 44

sleep, 9, 31, 32, 63, 83, 84, 85, 90, 96, 97, 98, 112

sleep loss, as sign of stress, 93

social commitments, 72

social media, as time-waster, 115, 120

social media, limiting use of, 28

social multitasking, 76

spam emails, 45

spare time, 71

specific goals, 53

starring emails, 44

stress, 17, 22, 28, 29, 30, 33, 35, 80, 83, 84, 85, 90, 92–94, 95, 99, 100, 109, 114, 118, 133

structure for working, 88

subfolders, for managing emails, 44

suicidal thoughts or actions, as sign of depression, 99

Sunday blues, 88

T

task, workplace definition of, 53

technology, 6, 15, 26, 27, 28, 135

time sucks, 71

time, value of, 11, 39

to-do lists, 21, 23, 27, 79

U

under-committing, 86

unplugging, 87

unwinding, 82, 84, 90

V

vacations, 11, 12, 83, 86, 89, 90, 91, 128

W

weekend planning, 85–86

weekends, 85–88

willpower, 106

work-schedule template, 37

working from home, 34, 63

workload, 47, 55, 74

workspace, managing clutter in your, 46

worrying to excess, as sign of anxiety, 99

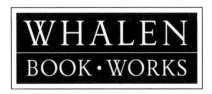

PUBLISHING PRACTICAL & CREATIVE NONFICTION

Whalen Book Works is a small, independent book publishing company based in Kennebunkport, Maine, that combines top-notch design, unique formats, and fresh content to create truly innovative gift books.

Our unconventional approach to bookmaking is a close-knit, creative, and collaborative process among authors, artists, designers, editors, and booksellers. We publish a small, carefully curated list each season, and we take the time to make each book exactly what it needs to be.

We believe in giving back. That's why we plant one tree for every ten books sold. Your purchase supports a tree in the Rocky Mountain National Park.

Get in touch!

Visit us at **WHALENBOOKS.COM**
or write to us at
68 North Street, Kennebunkport, ME 04046

TAKE YOUR CAREER
TO THE NEXT LEVEL!

OTHER TITLES IN THE SERIES INCLUDE:

Become a Manager,
ISBN 978-1-951511-08-1,
$11.95 US / $16.95 CAN

Business Etiquette,
ISBN 978-1-951511-09-8,
$11.95 US / $16.95 CAN

Career Success,
ISBN 978-1-951511-14-2,
$11.95 US / $16.95 CAN

Essential Sales Strategies,
ISBN 978-1-951511-12-8,
$11.95 US / $16.95 CAN

Marketing Fundamentals,
ISBN 978-1-951511-13-5,
$11.95 US / $16.95 CAN

Start a New Job Strong,
ISBN 978-1-951511-07-4,
$11.95 US / $16.95 CAN

Start Your Own Business,
ISBN 978-1-951511-11-1,
$11.95 US / $16.95 CAN